Die Hard
Die Hard (1988)
 131 min - Action | Thriller - 20 July 1988 (USA)
John McClane, officer of the NYPD, tries to save wife
Holly Gennaro and several others, taken hostage by
German terrorist Hans Gruber during a Christmas party
at the Nakatomi Plaza in Los Angeles.

Director: John McTiernan
Writers: Roderick Thorp (novel), Jeb Stuart
(screenplay)
Stars: Bruce Willis, Alan Rickman, Bonnie Bedelia

- From A Couple Of Average Joe's
Die Hard is one of those that comes along and hits on
all cylinders. The acting, the pacing, the action, the
humor, each piece of the movie essential for all the
other pieces to work. Making John McClane the "every
man" type of character who has to work his way through
a bad situation, where he is stuck in a 40-story
building, while bad guys hold people hostage in order
to steal money with no shoes, a gun and no help coming,
was unexpected for an action movie from the '80's where
most every movie of this type was a "super cop" or
"super soldier" wiping out platoons of military guys
and winning the day. This movie twisted that notion
and let us know that may be the good guy wasn't going
to win and that he could be injured. What makes Die
Hard so good is that it isn't just about the action or
the special effects, this is all about the characters
and the performance that McTiernan pulls out of each
actor to get their best.

Special, extra loud blanks were made for use in the
film to add to the "hyper-realism" director John
McTiernan was looking for. Unfortunately for Bruce
Willis, some of these blanks were used for the scene
where he kills a terrorist by shooting him through the
bottom of a table where the terrorist is standing. The
proximity of the gun to Willis' ear during this scene
caused permanent hearing loss for Willis.

The scene in which Gruber and McClane meet was inserted
into the script after Alan Rickman (Hans Gruber) was
found to be proficient at mimicking American accents.

The filmmakers had been looking for a way to have the two characters meet prior to the climax and capitalized on Rickman's talent.

The Nakatomi tower is actually the headquarters of 20th Century Fox. The company charged itself rent for the use of the then unfinished building.

The scene where McClane falls down a shaft was a mistake by the stuntman, who was supposed to grab the first vent, as it originally was planned. He slipped and continued to fall, but the shot was used anyway; it was edited together with one where McClane grabs the next vent down as he falls.

Director John McTiernan found it necessary to smash cut away from Hans Gruber's face whenever he

fired a gun, because of Alan Rickman's uncontrollable habit of flinching from the noise and muzzle flash. If you look at Rickman's face when he shoots Takagi, you can see him wincing.

John McTiernan was originally going to make Commando 2, but Arnold Schwarzenegger turned the role offer down. Commando 2 was transformed into this film; Schwarzenegger was the first actor offered the title role, but he again declined. Eventually Bruce Willis would get the part after it had been offered to Sylvester Stallone, Burt Reynolds, Harrison Ford, Mel Gibson and Richard Gere.

Joe and I do a podcast and for every podcast that we've done, Joe has some pretty great trivia facts. Those facts lead into what this book is all about - Entertainment Facts or Fiction. We've done our best to verify the facts for the movie trivia, but you just can't verify every thing, so there are facts in here that are duplicates with different information. That's done on purpose.

The way that this initial book is set up is the first part is generalized movie trivia and information and then we decided to do specific movie facts and trivia starting with Twilight Zone and Tales From The Crypt and movie through the Alien franchise and ending the book with some Die Hard trivia. Of course this is just the first in many books and we're not just focusing on movies. There will be a host of entertainment facts and trivia that will run from music, television, cartoons, books and even early radio shows.

We hope that you enjoy reading this book.

Be sure to follow us @mps5150 on Twitter for all the latest trivia tweets or you can visit our Facebook site www.facebook.com/diicastdotcom

We also do a podcast that you can hear through our page at www.acoupleofaveragejoes.com or on iTunes or through any podcast app that's available for your device. You can search for diicastdotcom or a couple of average joes.

A special thanks to my family - especially my mother and father for letting me pursue anything I wanted to pursue. it's taken some time, but I finally found the things I want to do.
Thank you to my brother and his wife and kids (Marc, Lora, William and Annah) and my sister (Heather and Gus and Jay) and Shellie and Craig and Shellies family and Dave Brandon and Deanna Eads and to all of those people that I am lucky enough to call my friends. Thank you all for putting up with my "dreamer" talk.

Of course, I can't forget Joe Speigle. With out him there is no podcast.

Joe - I wish to thank my my mother, grandmother and my kids William, Katelynn, Kora and Kendrick - I love you all.

There are a lot of movies and a lot of movie trivia out there. We didn't really know where to start so we thought we would just pick out a bunch of random movies that we love (and don't love) that have had some sort of impact on pop culture. The one cool surprise in this book is not a movie, but it's impact was the same. Tales From The Crypt is one of those TV shows that overstayed it's time on TV but the first several seasons were so good that it made people want to watch it just to see what they were going to do week after week. A modern day Twilight Zone but based on the popular E.C. Comics from the 1950's. The trivia for the television show was too good to pass up, that's why we included it in this volume. Here is the list of movies that we built this book on.
Die Hard, Die Hard 2 Die Harder, Die Hard Die Hard With A Vengeance, Live Free Or Die Hard, A Good Day To Die Hard, Alien, Aliens, Alien 3, Alien Resurrection, Alien Vs. Predator, Alien Vs. Predator 2 Requiem, Prometheus, Tales From The Crypt, Twilight Zone The Movie, and Random Movie Trivia.

Anyways, this is our big book of movie trivia volume 1. We hope you enjoy it!

All righty, hold your ears folks, it's SHOWTIME!

Let's DOOOOO THIS!

Hart Bochner's line "Hans... Bubby!" was ad-libbed.
Alan Rickman's quizzical reaction was genuine.

Bruce Willis received a then unheard of $5 million, a
fee that was OK'd by Fox President Rupert Murdoch.

The German that the terrorists speak is sometimes
grammatically incorrect. In the German version of the
film, the terrorists are not from Germany but from
"Europe". This has been fixed for the Special Edition
VHS and later home video releases. The only instances
of incorrect use of German are Alan Rickman's (Hans
Gruber) lines.

Only a couple of the actors who played the German
terrorists were actually German and only a couple more
could speak broken German. The actors were cast for
their menacing appearances rather than their
nationality. 9 of the 12 were over 6 feet tall.

The line "Yippee-ki-yay, motherfucker!" is used in all
Five Die Hard movies (this one, Die Hard 2 (1990), Die
Hard: With a Vengeance (1995), Live Free or Die Hard
(2007), {although a gunshot masks the 'fucker' part in
the PG13 cut} and A Good Day to Die Hard (2013)). It
also translates in Urdu to "here eat this." The line
was voted as the #96 of "The 100 Greatest Movie Lines"
by Premiere in 2007.

The scene where Bruce Willis and Alan Rickman meet up
was unrehearsed to create a greater feeling of
spontaneity between the two actors.

Bruce Willis personally recommended Bonnie Bedelia for
the role of his estranged wife.

When John McClane runs through the glass shards in his
'bare' feet after Hans has his men shoot out the glass
partitions in the computer room, Bruce Willis is in
fact wearing special 'rubber' shoes designed to look
like his own bare feet. One can in fact see this if
looking closely as his feet appear quite unnaturally
large in some of these crucial 'barefoot' scenes.

In the "Making of" Featurette for Die Hard: With a
Vengeance (1995), Reginald VelJohnson said that after
his appearances in the first two Die Hard films, he
would be frequently teased and joked at by friends and
people on the street for his character's obsession of
Twinkies, with some people even going so far as to buy
Twinkies and throwing them into his car while he was
inside, and saying things like "Oh we knew you wanted
some of those".

On Alan Rickman's first day of shooting he filmed the
scene where Hans Gruber first runs into John McClane.
He made a jump off the ledge about three feet high. He
injured his knee when he landed and damaged some
cartilage in his knee. He was told by his doctor not to
put any weight on that leg and he had to use crutches
for a week. For the rest of the scene where Hans Gruber
is standing and talking to John McClane, Alan Rickman
is standing on one leg for the entire time and has a
leg brace on under his pants.

When the bomb in the elevator shaft blows out the side of the building, the effect was accomplished by (a) collecting virtually every camera flashbulb of a particularly powerful type in the Los Angeles area and wiring them on the outside of the actual building to simulate the flash, and (b) by superimposing a shot of an actual explosive blowing a hole in the wall of an all-black miniature of the building at the appropriate location.

In the spring of 1987, producer Joel Silver and director John McTiernan attended a performance of the play Dangerous Liaisons, in which Alan Rickman played the evil Vicomte de Valmont. Immediately, Silver and McTiernan realized they had found Hans Gruber.

Much of the script was improvised due to the constant screenplay tweaks that were being made during filming.

In the German version the names and backgrounds of the German-born terrorists were changed into English forms (mostly into their British equivalents): Hans Gruber became Jack Gruber, Karl became Charlie, Heinrich turned into Henry etc... the new background depicted them as radical Irish activists having gone freelance and for profit rather than ideals. (This led to some odd plot holes in this movie and continuity problems with Die Hard: With a Vengeance (1995) where Gruber is remembered as having been German.) This was because German terrorism, especially by the Rote Armee Fraktion (the Red Army Faction), was still considered a sensitive issue by the German government in the 1980s.

Each film in the Die Hard series contains a key scene involving an elevator.

There are two FBI Agent Johnsons and a Harvey Johnson who were characters in the film. This is an in-joke aimed at co-star Reginald VelJohnson.

Deputy Chief Robinson says that John McClane (Bruce Willis) "could be a fucking bartender for all we know" (because of McClane's claim to be able to "spot a phony ID"). Prior to becoming a well-known actor, Willis was a bartender.

Bruce Willis was also shooting Moonlighting (1985) concurrently which accounts for why nearly all of McClane's scenes take place at night. Willis would shoot his TV series during the day and then come to the Fox lot in the evening to work on this film.

There are two references to the Japanese naval attack on Pearl Harbor on he 7th December 1941. The first occurs when John McClane questions whether the Japanese celebrate Christmas. Takagi replies "We're flexible, Pearl Harbor didn't work out so we got you with tape decks". The second is the breaking of the code key for the vault. The password "Akagi" (Red Castle in English) is the name of one of the Japanese aircraft carriers which carried out the strike on Pearl Harbor.

Ironically, Bruce Willis, sneered at for being an all-American hero by the head German terrorist, is actually more German than most of the villains; Alan Rickman is English and Alexander Godunov was Russian. Bruce Willis was born on March 19th 1955 in West Germany to an American father and a German mother.

The fireball in the elevator shaft was shot with real pyrotechnics using a miniature shaft; the camera speed had to vary over the length of the shot because otherwise the fireball would appear to change speed as it moved up the forced-perspective model. The effects people weren't sure exactly at what rate to vary the speed, so they rigged a manual variable-speed control and did several takes changing the speed at different rates and then picked the one that looked best.

The character of John McClane had not been fully realized until almost half way through production when John McTiernan and Bruce Willis decided that he was a man who did not like himself very much, but was doing the best he could in a bad situation.

At the suggestion of director John McTiernan, Ludwig van Beethoven's Ode to Joy (Ninth Symphony, Fourth Movement) is the musical theme of the terrorists. Hans Gruber, the terrorist leader, even hums it at one point in the movie (while he is on the elevator with Mr. Takagi). Film composer Michael Kamen at first thought it was a "sacrilege" to use Beethoven in an action movie, telling McTiernan: "I will make mincemeat out of Wagner or Strauss for you, but why Beethoven?" McTiernan replied that Ode to Joy had been the theme of the ultra-violence in Stanley Kubrick's A Clockwork Orange (1971). Kamen, a Kubrick fan, then agreed.

This was based on a book by Roderick Thorp entitled "Nothing Lasts Forever" - a sequel to another book entitled "The Detective", which in 1968 was made into a film starring Frank Sinatra. Because of a clause in Sinatra's contract for The Detective (1968) which gave him the right to reprise his role in a sequel, he was actually the first person offered the McClane role, even though he was 73 years old at the time. Also, Coincidentally, Bruce Willis made his movie debut in The First Deadly Sin (1980) walking out of a bar as Sinatra walks into it.

Clint Eastwood originally owned the rights to the novel "Nothing Lasts Forever" on which the film is based, and planned to star in the film around the early 1980s.

It is often said that Bruce Willis's lines during the scene when he pulls the glass out of his feet were ad-libbed. Indeed, it is said that upon learning this, Terry Gilliam cast Willis as the lead in Twelve Monkeys (1995). However when comparing the original script, it appears that Willis only veered very slightly from the original written dialog.

In the making-of featurette, director John McTiernan revealed that a vast majority of the exterior shots of the building showing explosions were real, full-scale explosions set off in and around the actual building.

The LAPD officer who gives medical attention to Sgt. Powell following the terrorists shooting up his car is actor Anthony Peck, who also plays NYPD Detective Ricky Walsh in Die Hard: With a Vengeance (1995).

Bruce Willis was the sixth choice for the main character. It originally went to Arnold Schwarzenegger, then Sylvester Stallone, then Burt Reynolds, then Richard Gere, then Harrison Ford, then Mel Gibson before Willis got it.

The firearms used in the film are, as in most action films, real firearms modified to function with blanks. Although modern small arms ammunition is intended to have minimum muzzle flash, director John McTiernan wanted vivid, "exaggerated realism" in the muzzle flashes. Weapons specialist Michael Papac hand fabricated some blanks that were so powerful that the standard firearms modifications weren't workable.

Papac had to specially modify the firearms involved. Special effects coordinator Al Di Sarro said of these blanks that 'in the world of blanks, there are loads that are not so loud and loads that are deafening', and these were deafening. These blanks did cause some cast members, notably Alan Rickman, to flinch. Furthermore, normally most sound effects come from a studio library of sound effects. Sound designer Richard Shorr didn't want to use these clips as modern sound equipment would show their age, as some of them were recorded in the 1950s. To resolve this and further the "exaggerated realism", the sound crew took the appropriate firearms to a firing range in Texas and recorded them being fired with live ammunition.

In the original script, the action took place over three days, but John McTiernan was inspired to have it take place over a single night by Shakespeare's A Midsummer Night's Dream.

The office interiors were designed to resemble Fallingwater, a house designed by architect Frank Lloyd Wright.

Bruce Willis' exhaustion from his schedule (he was also shooting Moonlighting (1985) forced Steven E. de Souza to beef up the roles of the other characters, giving characters like Al Powell, Ellis, Argyle, and Richard Thornburg more personality and screen time.

The original release poster for the film did not feature Bruce Willis' likeness, just the building (pre-release promo posters did show Willis). The producers originally thought it might deter non-Willis fans from seeing the movie. Posters were later altered after the early box office success.

Hans Gruber was also the name of an adversary in Our Man Flint (1966) with James Coburn.

The addresses and phone numbers depicted on the LAPD dispatch's computer for the Nakatomi plaza management are the actual numbers for management of Fox Plaza, where the film was shot.

When talking to Powell on CB, McClane tells him, "They have missiles, automatic weapons and enough plastic explosives to orbit Arnold Schwarzenegger." Arnold Schwarzenegger was originally considered for the role of McClane. Schwarzenegger and Bruce Willis, who are now both known as for making action movies with a dark humor, later became good friends.

EASTER EGG: On Disc 2 of the 2-Disc DVD (the Special Features Disc), from the first selection of the menu, push right on the remote control, and a dot on the top of the menu (which resembles the rooftop of the Nakatomi building) will light up. Select it, and the menu will "explode" and the words "THERE GOES FOX HOME ENTERTAINMENT!" will appear when the explosion clears.

When they first meet Takagi tells John McClane that 'Pearl Harbor didn't work out so we hit you with stereos'. James Shigeta who played Takagi also played Vice Admiral Chiuichi Nagumo, one of the architects of the attack on Pearl Harbor in the film The Battle of Midway (1976).

Sam Neill turned down the role of Hans Gruber.

Bruce Willis took the role of John McClane after it had been turned down by Robert De Niro. Willis had just been turned down to play the Charles Grodin role opposite De Niro in Midnight Run (1988). Ironically both films eventually opened the same weekend.

The building used in the movie was designed by William L. Pereira, and was one of his last projects before his death in 1985.

The film's ending had not been finalized by the time filming had begun. One result is that the truck depicted as transporting the terrorists to the building is too small to house the ambulance that was later revealed to be inside it. Other scenes also lacked context: the building's computer room was built before anyone knew what it would be used for.

The character of Hans Gruber is rumored to be based on author Roderick Thorp's father, a known tyrant amongst friends and family.

The Hungarian title is "Give your life expensive", the title of the sequel is "Your life is more expensive", and the third part is "The life is always expensive"

Michael Madsen was considered for the role of John McClane.

The odd looking gun that Karl uses in the film is a Steyr AUG, an Austrian made assault rifle.

On the Blu-ray Disc commentary, Production Designer Jackson De Govia notes the company name on the truck in which the "raiders" (as he calls them) arrive. It says, "Pacific Courier" - a joke, since it means "Messenger of Peace". DeGovia used the same name and graphic on the truck that gets blown up at the start of Die Hard: With a Vengeance (1995).

John McTiernan did not want the villains to be terrorists, considering them too mean. He chose to avoid the terrorists' politics in favor of making them thieves in pursuit of monetary gain, believing it would make the film more suitable for summer entertainment.

When the police dispatcher tells Sergeant Powell to investigate the Nakatomi building, she tells him it is a "Code 2". This refers to an urgent incident where sirens are not to be used.

In Spain, the title was translated into "Crystal Jungle." In Poland it became "The Glass Trap," which sounds and fits very well in that country. The original title is hard to translate correctly, as it would sound like: "It is hard to kill him" or "He dies slowly." The same titles are used for the sequels even though they do not relate well to the sequels.

John McTiernan turned the script down several times. He felt it was a nasty piece of work. When he was finally persuaded to take on the assignment, he was able to lighten some of the film's darker edges.

The bridge shown in Takagi's office is a work of Frank Lloyd Wright for the Bay Area in 1949.

The centerfold that John McClane sees and ultimately uses as a point of reference while navigating his way from the elevator shaft to the air vent is that of Playboy Playmate Pamela Stein (November 1987). Another Playboy Playmate, May 1982 star Kym Malin, has a small role in the picture as the hostage who is originally discovered by the terrorists having sex with another party goer, and a third, July 1988 Playmate of the Month Terri Lynn Doss, plays the woman at the airport who runs past McClane to hug another arriving passenger.

Each of the first 3 'Die Hard' films has a connection and/or reference to at least 1 of the 3 countries of Northern Europe: Norway, Sweden, and Finland. Here, in the first one, it is during the news broadcast when the psychologist mentions "Helsinki Syndrome" (which is actually "Stockholm Syndrome") and the subsequent mentions of Sweden (whose capital is Stockholm) and Finland (whose capital is Helsinki).

Before reporter Richard Thornburg hears Sgt Powell's call for backup over the radio he is discussing dinner reservations with a woman, saying "of course I can get a table, Wolfgang is a close personal friend of mine". This refers to Wolfgang Puck and his Sunset Strip restaurant "Spago", which opened in 1982.

A full 18 minutes elapse before first gunshot in Die Hard.

Charles Bronson was considered for the role of John McClane but he was under contract with Cannon Films at the time.

Bruce Willis and Demi Moore tied the knot at the Golden Nugget hotel in Las Vegas during this shoot, Moore having recently broken her engagement to actor Emilio Estevez. Little Richard presided over the ceremony and former brat packer Ally Sheedy was a bridesmaid.

Don Johnson and Richard Dean Anderson, both established action stars in television, were considered for the role of John McClane.

Due to the tourist interest in the Fox Plaza building in L.A., people are now forbidden from taking photos outside the building.

Though Heinrich is supposedly German, the cigarettes John McClane picks up in his pockets are French-made Gauloises. Fittingly, these used to be army-issue and are known for their strong, harsh taste.

In this film you can see that John McClane has a tattoo but in all the other die hard films this tattoo is not present

The Serbian, Croatian and Bosnian translation of the title is "Umri Muski" ("Die Like A True Man"; literary: "Die Manly"). The pirated VHS translation back in 1988 was "Skupo Prodaj Svoju Kozu" ("Sell Your Skin At High Price").

The music being played at the corporate gathering at the beginning of the film is from the first movement of Johann Sebastian Bach's Third Brandenberg Concerto.

The scene which McClain embraces Holly, when Hans Gruber is killed had to be re-shot 4 times because Bruce Willis kept making Bonnie Bedelia crack up with laughter. The 1st take he made his co-star unintentionally laugh when he says "Didn't want to do this" and said "Ye!" in a funny voice. In the 2nd take, Willis made Bedelia laugh again when he did an impression of a monkey and in the 3rd take, he broke into song by singing "Paris in Spring" by Mary Ellis, which the whole crew laughed.

The entire Nakatomi building was supposed to be managed by a supercomputer and the scenes where McClane is trapped in an office and Gruber orders the windows to be shot out are supposed to be the computer room. The large dark object is the computer, modeled after an ETA-10 supercomputer. It is a model and a bit larger than the actual computer which was thought to look too small. The fiberglass model was later used by ETA as part of the marketing for the ETA range of supercomputers.

In Nakatomi building's vault is supposed to be kept, amongst other pieces of art, the Edgar Degas' painting "Ecole de dance" (1873) (as shown when the "terrorists" finally break the last lock). Actually, it's in Corcoran Museum of Arts in Washington DC.

When Powell circles the Nakatomi parking lot, McClane looks on, saying "Who's driving this car, Stevie Wonder?" As Argyle waits in the limo parked in the garage, "Skeletons" by Stevie Wonder plays on the stereo.

Richard Gere was considered for the role of John McClane.

This movie, set during Christmas time in Los Angeles, has the lead terrorist named Hans Gruber. The Christmas Carol "Silent Night" was composed in Salzburg, Austria by Franz Gruber, a school teacher and church organist. He wrote the melody for a guitar arrangement at the request of the 6-stanza poem's author Fr. Joseph Mohr, a Roman Catholic priest and assistant pastor at St. Nicholas Church, who wrote it in 1816. Mohr and Gruber first sang the song "Stille Nacht" at midnight mass on December 24, 1818, while Mohr played his guitar.

Nick Nolte was the first one to turn down the lead.

The terrorists arrive in a truck that is green with a white top with "Pacific Courier" on the side. Ironically, "Pacific Courier" translates to mean "Bringer of Peace".

Al Pacino was considered for the role of John McClane but turned it down.

When John is looking up his wife's location on the computer in the lobby, he finds her name listed as "GENNARO, HOLLY". If you watch the scene in slow motion, you will see her last name change to "GENNERO, HOLLY" after John touches her name on the screen.

Bruce Willis worked with some of the actors who were considered for his role as John McClane later on. He worked with Don Johnson in an episode of Miami Vice, Richard Gere in The Jackal, Michael Madsen in Sin City, and Arnold Schwarzenegger and Sylvester Stallone in The Expendables.

Hart Bochner, who plays Harry Ellis, is the son of actor Lloyd Bochner, who co-starred with 'Frank Sinatra' (QV) in The Detective (1968), based on the novel by author Roderick Thorp. Die Hard (1988) is based on Thorp's novel "Nothing Lasts Forever", the sequel to "The Detective."

Rick Ducommun: Actor that plays the worker in man hole that radios to shut the power down also played the man that has his pool set on fire and gets shot by Milo in the last boyscout also starring Bruce Willis.

The Fox Plaza is represented three-dimensionally in Google Earth in 3d buildings mode.

Bruce Willis is left-handed, therefore John McClane is portrayed as being left-handed. The Beretta 92F used in the film was modified to better accommodate Willis being a southpaw.

In a scene where Bruce Willis had to shoot under a small table, he suffered two thirds hearing loss in his left ear. This was due to the extra loud blanks fired in a small restrictive space.

In the first scene where the two helicopter gunships appear, the lighted building letters in the background reads: Agfa-Gevaert.

John McTiernan: [teddy bear] McClane has a teddy bear for his family. The same bear is seen at the end of The Hunt for Red October (1990).

For the shot where Hans Gruber falls from the top of the building, Alan Rickman was actually falling from a 21-foot high model. He was holding on to a stunt man and falling on to an air bag. To get the right reaction, the stunt man dropped Rickman on the count of two, not three.

The original script called for terrorists to hijack the building, and for a super-hero cop to stop them. Director John McTiernan modified the script to change the bad guys into robbers pretending to be terrorists so that the audience could enjoy their intention of grabbing a load of money. He felt having terrorists as the villains would make the movie less enjoyable and give it a political angle, which he wanted to avoid. McTiernan also changed the hero, John McClane, into an everyday, flawed man that rises to the occasion in dire circumstances. He felt the audience would identify more with him than with a "super-cop".

Hans Gruber's fall was filmed at 300 frames per second.

The Roderick Thorp book "Nothing Lasts Forever," which serves as the basis for this movie, was actually a sequel to the book and film The Detective (1968), with Frank Sinatra as Joe Leland. Surprisingly, few of the book's details are changed. Originally, a much older

Leland (changed to McClane) was visiting his daughter, Steffie Leland Gennaro, who worked for the Klaxxon oil company. Takagi was originally a VP of sales named Rivers. Harry Ellis, Al Powell, and Dwayne Robinson were essentially the same, but the FBI was not involved. Hans Gruber was originally Anton "Little Tony" Gruber, while Hans was the name of Karl's brother. The purpose of the terrorist takeover was to allow the West German radical group to uncover an illegal arms shipment Klaxxon was making to a Chilean dictatorship. Finally, in the end scene (which was Christmas morning at 10 AM), Anton Gruber is shot by Leland and falls out the window, also catching a finger on Gennaro's watch, but in this case he pulls her out the window to her death.

The music cue when Powell shoots Karl at the end of the film was actually an unused track from James Horner's Academy Award-nominated score for Aliens (1986), another Fox film. Specifically, the music was originally intended for a scene near the end of the film, in which Ripley (Sigourney Weaver) battles with the alien queen on board the Sulaco. Instead, an earlier music cue was reused, leaving the cue available for this film. A second music cue, scored by John Scott for the film Man on Fire (1987), was also used. The music can be heard when McClane and Holly meet Powell at the end of the movie.

On-screen body count: 21. These include (in order) both Nakatomi security guards, Takagi, Tony, Heinrich, Marco, James and Alexander (both blown up at the same time), Ellis, Franco, Fritz, Uli, both agent Johnsons and the 4 other guys on the chopper, Eddie, Hans and Karl.

Powell shoots Karl a total of five times during the final scene outside the building.

Even though Arnold Schwarzenegger and Sylvester Stallone were considered for John McClane in Die Hard and it went to their pal Bruce Willis, who they later worked with in the expendables movies. There is a reference to Die Hard in Expendables 2 where Arnold says Bruce's line "yippie Kai yay" after Bruce says Arnold's line from Terminator, "I'll be back."

4 of the actors who were considered to be John McClane later appeared in the Expendables films which happen to be Arnold Schwarzenegger, Sylvester Stallone, Mel Gibson and Harrison Ford. Sly and Arnold appeared with Bruce Willis in the first two, but Bruce Willis was supposed to appear in the third one and didn't due to money problems. The third one had Mel Gibson and Harrison Ford replacing Bruce Willis. So Bruce missed the opportunity to work with Ford and Gibson.

"Die Hard" was Alan Rickman's feature film debut. That's right, Professor Snape, who's set to play Ronald Reagan in the upcoming film "The Butler," was first introduced to the big screen as the infamous Hans Gruber.

In the film, Deputy Chief Robinson (Paul Gleason) says that McClane (Willis) "could be a f*cking bartender for all we know" because of McClane's claim to be able to "spot a phony ID." Coincidentally, prior to acting, Willis was a bartender.

"Yippee-ki-yay, motherf*cker!" is said in all five "Die Hard" movies. Willis recently shared that it originated as a joke: "It was a throwaway. I was just trying to crack up the crew and I never thought it was going to be allowed to stay in the film."

On the special features of the "Die Hard: With a Vengeance" DVD, Reginald VelJohnson, who plays Sgt. Powell, said that after his appearances in the first two "Die Hard" films, he would frequently be teased for his character's obsession with Twinkies. Some people would go as far as to throw Twinkies into his car while he was inside, saying things like "Oh, we knew you wanted some of those."

Bruce Willis received a then-unheard-of $5 million for the film, a fee that was approved by Fox President Rupert Murdoch.

"Die Hard" was based on Roderick Thorp's book "Nothing Lasts Forever," the sequel to his novel "The Detective," which was made into a 1968 film starring Frank Sinatra. Since a clause in Sinatra's contract gave him the right to reprise his role in a sequel, he was the first person offered the role of McClane even though he was 73 years old at the time. Coincidentally, Willis made his feature film debut in "The First Deadly Sin," walking out of a bar as Sinatra walked into it.

In the version of "Die Hard" released in Germany, the terrorists are not specified as German, but are said to be "from Europe."

At the suggestion of McTiernan, Beethoven's Ode to Joy
from "Symphony No. 9" became the musical theme of the
terrorists, and eventually all the "Die Hard" films.
Hans Gruber even hums it at one point in "Die Hard"
while he is on the elevator with Mr. Takagi (James
Shigeta). McTiernan wanted to use it since it had been
the theme of the ultra-violence depicted in Stanley
Kubrick's "A Clockwork Orange."

Hart Bochner's line "Hans... Bubby!" in the film was
ad-libbed. Alan Rickman's quizzical reaction was
genuine.

This movie, set during Christmas time in Los Angeles,
has the lead terrorist named Hans Gruber. The Christmas
Carol "Silent Night" was composed in Salzburg, Austria
by Franz Gruber, a school teacher and church organist.
He wrote the melody for a guitar arrangement at the
request of the 6-stanza poem's author Fr. Joseph Mohr,
a Roman Catholic priest and assistant pastor at St.
Nicholas Church, who wrote it in 1816. Mohr and Gruber
first sang the song "Stille Nacht" at midnight mass on
December 24, 1818, while Mohr played his guitar.

The character of Hans Gruber is rumored to be based on
author Roderick Thorp's father, a known tyrant amongst
friends and family.

When talking to Powell on CB, McClane tells him, "They
have missiles, automatic weapons and enough plastic
explosives to orbit Arnold Schwarzenegger." Arnold
Schwarzenegger was originally considered for the role
of McClane. Schwarzenegger and Bruce Willis, who are
now both known for making action movies with a dark
humor, later became good friends.

The purpose of the terrorist takeover was to allow the
West German radical group to uncover an illegal arms
shipment Klaxxon was making to a Chilean dictatorship.
Finally, in the end scene (which was Christmas morning
at 10 AM), Anton Gruber is shot by Leland and falls out
the window, also catching a finger on Gennaro's watch,

but in this case he pulls her out the window to her
death.

Die Hard 2 (1990)
 124 min - Action | Thriller - 4 July 1990 (USA)
John McClane, officer of the N.Y.P.D. and hero of the
Nakatomi Hostage Crisis, attempts to avert disaster as
rogue military officials seize control of Dulles
International Airport in Washington, D.C.

Director: Renny Harlin
Writers: Walter Wager (novel), Steven E. de Souza
(screenplay),
Stars: Bruce Willis, William Atherton, Bonnie Bedelia

-A Couple Of Average Joe's
Die Hard 2: Die Harder is a decent follow up to the
first film but it lacks the excitement and originality
of the first movie. McClane is waiting for his wife at
Dulles Airport where they are going to spend Christmas
with the relatives and then things go wrong when a
rogue contingent of mercenaries decide to take over the
airport so that they can rescue their comrade in arms
from a military prison plane. The movie in and of
itself would have been fine as a non-Die Hard movie but
it seemed that, at the time, the studio really wanted
to capitalize on the first one and rushed this movie
into production. John McClane being the guy in the
wrong place at the wrong time is the theme to all the
Die Hard movies but, this movie seems to take that to
the extreme. While the action parts of the movie are
well done, the plot, the pacing and the fun from the
first one seems to be lost.

This is Bruce Willis's least favorite film of the "Die
Hard" series.

According to John Leguizamo in his autobiography, his
role was intended to be much larger until the
filmmakers realized how short he was. His part was cut
down to one line which was dubbed by someone else.
However, he got his way years later in Executive
Decision (1996), another picture produced by Joel
Silver and often described as 'Die Hard on a Plane'.

Renny Harlin made sure that the scene where Major Grant
says to McClane that he is "the wrong guy in the wrong
place at the wrong time", with McClane responding

"Yeah, story of my life", ended up in the movie's trailer, because it perfectly summed up McClane's character.

In the original Die Hard (1988), John McClane only had a few scripted one-liners. However, Bruce Willis ad-libbed so many one liners and audiences liked them so much that in this sequel (and the next one), more gags were added and Willis was told he could ad-lib as many more as he saw fit.

SERIES TRADEMARK: The line "Yipee-ki-yay, motherfucker!"

Minnesota was originally picked for location filming, but there was no snow, so filming was moved to Michigan.

The General is from Val Verde, the fictitious Latin-American country used in Commando (1985).

The scenes with Bruce Willis running through tunnels under the airport were filmed at a water treatment facility near Los Angeles. The facility has miles of underground tunnels, and was also used in Live Free or Die Hard (2007), doubling as the Woodlawn Social Security Administration building.

The scene where McClane climbs the ladder from the service tunnels up onto the runway and then nearly gets run over by Esperanza's plane was filmed from eight different locations: - Granada Hills, California (McClain in the tunnel and climbing up the ladder) - Los Angeles, California (Close-ups of Esperanza inside the plane's cockpit) - Mojave Desert, California (Head-on view of plane in the sky on approach) - Alpena, Michigan (Exterior shot of the grating door on the runway) - San Francisco, California (Rear shot of plane on approach with runway lights in the background) - Sault Ste. Marie, Michigan (Plane after just landed rushing towards the screen) - Lake Tahoe, California (Plane rushing towards McClane in the foreground) - Denver, Colorado (Plane rushing towards McClane as seen from behind the front landing gear).

Black & Decker paid to have its cordless drill featured in a scene with Bruce Willis. When the scene was cut, the company sued 20th Century Fox in the first-ever product placement lawsuit for a film. The $150,000 claim was settled out of court.

John McTiernan had planned to direct this film, but could not because of his commitment to directing The Hunt for Red October (1990).

Major Grant's commando team is referred to as 'Blue Light'. This was the name of a real life US military anti-terrorist team formed within the US Special Forces in the 1970s. It was eventually replaced by the Delta Force who recruited personnel from the entire army rather than just Green Berets.

Based on the novel "58 Minutes" by Walter Wager. Hence the French title "58 Minutes Pour Vivre" ("58 Minutes To Live").

Denver was unseasonably snowless during the shooting of the snowstorm scenes and a fair amount of snow had to be created artificially.

This film was shipped to theaters as "wet prints" - an industry term meaning that it was just barely completed before its release date.

Most of the interior airport scenes were filmed in the Tom Bradley International Terminal at Los Angeles International airport.

The only movie in the Die Hard series that contains neither a plot nor a subplot pertaining to the acquisition of money, gold, bearer bonds, or any form of currency by the bad guys.

The Russian title for "Die Hard" in all of the three movies is, "A Hard Nut to Crack".

The confrontation between Bruce Willis and William Sadler on the airplane's wing took several nights to shoot. Huge fans were used to blow in the fake snow in the background because of lack of real snow.

In the "Making of" Featurette for Die Hard: With a Vengeance (1995), actor William Sadler (Col. Stuart) said that for this movie, his favorite part pertaining to his character was when Col. Stuart crashes the Windsor Air plane by pretending to be someone from the tower.

The subplot involving Esperanza being turned over to the US government is a reference to the real-life Panamanian general, Manuel Noriega, who was overthrown for brutality and drug trafficking in Panama in the 1980s.

It was Renny Harlin's idea that William Sadler, the film's main villain be introduced naked doing martial arts exercises during the film's opening sequence. He would later say that it was "an effective, but unusual way to introduce a character".

In Die Hard (1988), Sgt. Al Powell is humming along with the song "Let It Snow!" sung by Vaughn Monroe; the same song plays both at the end of this film and Die Hard.

All the airplane landing equipment used by the mercenaries in the church is close to the real equipment used in actual air traffic control towers, but simplified for the film's dramatic and action effects.

Although the movie was filmed using a fictitious airport and/or other airports with stood in for Dulles Int'l Airport, the movie posters along with the VHS and DVD covers for the movie show a picture of the actual Dulles Airport itself.

Some of the shots of the airport (interior and exterior) were filmed at the old Stapleton Airport in Denver, Colorado. Also, the external shots of the church were filmed in Highland Lake, just north of Denver.

Actors Dennis Franz and Robert Costanzo, who played Carmine and Vito Lorenzo, would work together again in 1993, during the first season of ABC's NYPD Blue (1993), when Costanzo would play mobster Alphonse Giardella, with whom Franz's Sipowicz had an ongoing feud that would end in the detective's near-execution in the pilot episode.

Renny Harlin edited this film and The Adventures of Ford Fairlane (1990) at the same time because of the relatively short post-production period for both films. The films were then released one month apart.

The first time Holly McClane is seen on the plane, the woman sitting next to her is reading a magazine advertising the VHS release of Lethal Weapon. Both the

first two Die Hard movies and the Lethal Weapon
franchise were produced by producer Joel Silver.

In the "Making of" featurette for Die Hard: With a
Vengeance (1995), Reginald VelJohnson said that after
his appearances in the first two "Die Hard" films, he
would be frequently teased and joked at by friends and
people on the street for his character's obsession with
Twinkies, with some people even going so far as to buy
Twinkies and throw them into his car while he was
inside, and saying things like, "Oh we knew you wanted
some of those".

There is a war reference in each of the first three Die
Hard films. This film's references include Marvin
mentioning both Iwo Jima and Pearl Harbor and the
Commando team reminiscing about Grenada.

The music heard in the film's theatrical trailer is
"Ode to Joy" from Ludwig van Beethoven's Ninth
Symphony, which is heard throughout the first Die Hard
(1988) film in Michael Kamen's score.

Was supposed to be filmed at Moses Lake, Washington but, like Minnesota, there was no snow.

Cast members Bruce Willis, William Sadler, and Fred Dalton Thompson all appeared in the first season (1988-89) of "Roseanne" (1988-1997).

The aircraft that General Esperanza arrives on is a Fairchild C-123K Provider. This is a twin engine propeller airplane modified to appear with four jet engines for the film. The pods for the J-85 jet booster engines are still visible under the wings between the mock-up jet engines.

The Polish title for "Die Hard" in all of the three movies is "The Glass Trap", as a reference to the first movie located in a glass skyscraper.

Carmine Lorenzo (Dennis Franz) asks McClane if he thinks he is "playing John Wayne". In the original Die Hard, Hans Gruber (Alan Rickman) also compares McClane to John Wayne.

Robert Patrick, along with Jai Courtney, both share the distinction of appearing in the Die Hard franchise and the Terminator franchise. Robert Patrick appears in Die Hard 2 (1990) as a henchman and in Terminator 2: Judgement Day (1991) as the T-1000. Jai Courtney appears as Jack McClane in A Good Day to Die Hard (2013) and as Kyle Reese in Terminator Genisys (2015).

Until the fifth film, this is the only Die Hard film with no action scene in an elevator sequence.

The 747 plane that General Esperanza, Colonel Stuart, and the other terrorists use to try to escape in bears the livery colors of Evergreen International Air Cargo Lines, but with the company name whited out.

EASTER EGG: On Disc 2 of the 2-Disc DVD (the Special Features disc), push right on the remote control from the last menu selection, and the "stair rail" will light up. Select it to display credits for the creators of the Special Features disc.

The Spanish title for "Die Hard" in all of the three movies is "The Glass Jungle", as a reference to the first Die Hard (1988) movie being set in a glass skyscraper.

Each film in the Die Hard series contains a key scene involving an elevator.

Each of the first 3 'Die Hard' films has a connection and/or reference to at least 1 of the 3 countries of Northern Europe: Norway, Sweden, and Finland. Here, in the second one, the director, Renny Harlin, is from Finland, and the musical piece "Finlandia" by Finnish composer Jean Sibelius is featured twice during the film.

At the end of the movie, shows the wide shot of NEA L-1011 from the rear clearly shows a FAA registration number "N765BE" formerly operated by All Nippon Airways, Hawaiian Airlines and Rich International Airlines. The aircraft was later scrapped in 2004. One of the scene shows the NEA livery is slowly fading off. Looking at the forward section of the L-1011 aircraft, near at the NEA logo, the name of the former operator HAWAIIAN can be seen.

The scenes filmed in Denver had to have snow machines brought from a local ski resort with truck loads of ice every night, during the day it would all melt. Stapleton international airport, where some external, and internal shots were filmed, shut down at night because of noise abatement laws.

In the begninng of the movie, McClane kills a guy named
Sgt. Oswald Cochran who was an American advisor in
Honduras and was ruled dead after a helicopter accident
on 5-11-88 (May 11, 1988).

Renny Harlin: [Finland] "Finlandia" by Jean Sibelius
is used in some scenes.

Local transmission of The Simpsons (1989) shown on the
plane to "calm the passengers" is the episode [The
Simpsons: There's No Disgrace Like Home (1990)] where
Dr. Monroe allows each family member to use shock
therapy on other family members. Later, Holly McClane
shocks Richard Thornburg in the lavatory.

Several scenes were filmed but cut from the final
release of the film: An extended version of the scene
when McClane enters the terminal, featuring shots of a
children's choir singing Christmas carols (the audio of
the choir singing still remains in the final cut, but
only heard in the background), A scene of two of the
terrorists killing off two painters and stealing their
truck as well as their uniforms (to pose as painters
later in the Skywalk SWAT team ambush scene). An
extended version of the scene where McClane first meets
up with Marvin the janitor, and finally an extended
scene of Marvin showing McClane the best way to access
the tunnels to get to the runways, which includes a
scene where McClane has to walk carefully across a
narrow beam over a hot boiler. All of these cut scenes
can be viewed in the Deleted Scenes section of the
Special Features disc.

Die Hard: With a Vengeance (1995)
131 min - Action | Adventure | Thriller - 19 May
1995 (USA)
John McClane and a Harlem store owner are targeted by
German terrorist Simon Gruber in New York City, where
he plans to rob the Federal Reserve Building.

Director: John McTiernan
Writers: Jonathan Hensleigh, Roderick Thorp (certain
original characters)
Stars: Bruce Willis, Jeremy Irons, Samuel L. Jackson

-A Couple Of Average Joe's
Die Hard 3 sees the return of John McTiernan to the
role of director and that's a good thing for this
franchise. McTiernan brings back the pacing and action
and humor from the first movie, while providing us with
a new villian, Simon Gruber, Hans Gruber's brother who
is seeking his revenge against McClane while at the
same time, he's trying to rob the Federal Reserve Bank
of New York. What's good about this movie is the
addition of Samuel L. Jackson as McClane's conscience.
He's the voice of reason through out the movie while
McClane goes on a crazy chase across New York to try
and stop Simon Gruber from stealing money. What makes
this movie good is that McTiernan doesn't shy away from
the stories elements, McClane, Grubner and money. The
basics of the first Die Hard.

Jonathan Hensleigh was actually detained by the FBI
after completing the script for the film because he
knew extensive information about the Federal Gold
Reserve in downtown Manhattan. Hensleigh stated that he
got all the information from an article written in the
New York Times.

Originally titled "Simon Says" (where Zeus was scripted
as a woman) and was considered by Joel Silver as the
fourth sequel to Lethal Weapon (1987). FOX, however,
did not agree to sell the script to Joel Silver.

The sandwich board that Bruce Willis wore while filming
in Harlem was originally blank, rather than text, to
ensure no one was offended by the racist message. The
"I Hate Niggers" was added with CGI in post-production.

Some television broadcasts use an alternate version
where the sign reads "I hate everybody", which is
sometimes erroneously said to be the original version
of the sign used for filming, but this too was added
with CGI in post-production.

Director John McTiernan acknowledged the errors
concerning the gold in the dump trucks and its
respective weight. McTiernan and Samuel L. Jackson were
permitted to lift a genuine bar of gold to get a feel
of how heavy gold really was.

When Zeus Carver picks up the gold bar at the Federal
Reserve, he says "Damn, this is heavy" A standard gold
bar kept at the Federal Reserve weighs approximately 25
lbs.

Although Bruce Willis and Samuel L. Jackson had both
appeared in Loaded Weapon 1 (1993) and Pulp Fiction
(1994), this is the first movie where the two appear
on-screen together.

Samuel L. Jackson's look in the film was Jackson's idea
after he'd done extensive research on his character by
studying books on Malcolm X.

The studio told screenwriter Jonathan Hensleigh to
remove the scenes with McClane walking around Harlem
wearing a sign that says, "I hate niggers." They
allowed him to keep the scene when he threatened to
take the script to another studio.

After their run across New York, Zeus (Samuel L. Jackson) accuses McClain (Bruce Willis) of being out of shape for a cop. (They took a cab, they didn't run. They are exciting the cab when McClain says "Cheer up. Things could be worse. I was working on a nice fat suspension. Smokin cigarettes and watching Captain Kangaroo.") In the film Pulp Fiction (1994), which stars both Willis and Jackson, the song "Flowers On the Wall" where this quote is from is playing on the radio in Willis' characters car just before he runs it into Marsellus Wallace outside his apartment.

Although he wasn't hired for the film, Alan Rickman is still credited as playing Hans Gruber (in McClane's flashback, using stock footage from Die Hard (1988)).

Sean Connery was John McTiernan's very first choice for the role of Simon Gruber. He turned down the role, saying that he didn't want to play such a diabolical villain.

The sex scene between Jeremy Irons and Sam Phillips was added in at the last minute because John McTiernan knew that the film would get an R rating and he might as well put a sex scene in.

In Greek mythology, Zeus was a god who summoned lightning and thunder. In this movie, Zeus Carver is an electrician.

When the bomb goes off in the Bonwit Teller department store, there is an "Atlantic Courier" truck parked in front of the store that gets flipped over. In Die Hard (1988), Hans Gruber and the other terrorists arrive at Nakatomi Plaza in a "Pacific Courier" truck.

In the DVD commentary, Jonathan Hensleigh says that the first hour of the film is his original "Simon Says" script word for word. He only changed the characters from the script, so that it would actually feel a part of the "Die Hard" series.

As in the previous Die Hard (1988), the German spoken in this movie is mostly grammatically incorrect. A few lines are so wrong that they have to be considered gibberish (most notably the exchange of the fake cops, who are given the briefcase bomb by Zeus (Samuel L. Jackson)). In the German release, however, all of the lines that were German in the original movie are grammatically correct, fitting the context and some of the terrorists even have an East German accent.

Even though this is the third film in the Die Hard series, it is the first that takes place in the same city that John McClane is a police officer (New York). In the first movie he is in LA, and in the second he is in Washington, DC.

The park on top of the Wall Street station in the film was a vacant lot that was made into a park for the film. It was turned back into a vacant lot after filming was completed.

The chase scenes in the tunnel were filmed in New York City Water Tunnel Number 3, an unfinished aqueduct connecting the city to the Catskill Mountains in upstate New York.

Director John McTiernan considered either editing out the beginning bombing of the department store, or moving the release date back as they felt that the American public might still be sensitive to bombing due to closeness of dates of the Oklahoma City bombing of the Alfred P. Murray Federal Building.

In the scene where Zeus (Samuel L. Jackson) is trying to get out of going with McClane (Bruce Willis) on the trip across the city, he [Zeus] gets up, exclaiming, "I'm not jumping through hoops for some psycho! That's a white man with white problems, you deal with him! Let me know when he crosses 110th street." The line "Across 110th Street" is a reference to the film of the same name, whose main title was a pop hit, and was featured in the film Jackie Brown (1997), which also starred Samuel L. Jackson.

On the DVD commentary, screenwriter Jonathan Hensleigh says the idea for the film's plot came to him when he imagined what would happen if one of his childhood friends, who was injured after Hensleigh threw a rock at him, decided to seek revenge on him as an adult.

Sam Phillips Simons girlfriend never says a word.

Laurence Fishburne was the original choice to play Zeus Carver, but turned down the part. When he reconsidered the decision, Samuel L. Jackson was already cast.

Simon calls a radio announcer to report that there is a bomb in a school. The name of the announcer is Elvis Duran, an actual radio announcer on the station Z100 (100.3 FM).

The first "Die Hard" movie to be based on an original screenplay. Die Hard (1988) is based on the novel by Roderick Thorp, Die Hard 2 (1990) is based on a novel by Walter Wager and Live Free or Die Hard (2007) is based on an article by John Carlin.

When McClane boards the elevator at the Federal Reserve with Karl and the rest of Simon's men, during the casual conversation Karl is having with McClane, Karl refers to the elevator as the "lift". This would potentially betray Karl, who is trained in infiltration and disguised as a Federal Reserve guard, as being European and therefore a potential imposter since "lift" is the European term for elevator.

Sam Phillips, in real life a pop singer, was invited to test for the role based upon a photo from one of her CD covers.

The R2 DVD was originally released with a TV-like edit with all swearing removed and key scenes like the elevator gunfight cut out. The DVDs were all recalled then released as the original edit.

On the Die Hard (1988) Blu-ray Disc commentary, Production Designer Jackson De Govia notes the company name on the truck in which the "raiders" (as he calls them) arrive in the first movie. It says, "Pacific Courier" - a joke, because it means "Messenger of Peace". DeGovia used the same name and graphic on the truck that gets blown up at the start of *this* movie.

This is the only Die Hard film that John McClane didn't risk his life to save Holly or any one of his kids.

The producers planned to blow up the Hutchinson River Parkway tollbooth structure for a scene in the movie. The tolls were to be eliminated anyway, and then-Governor Mario Cuomo volunteered to push the switch. But opposition from local residents in close proximity and from other officials killed the idea.

The school kids "trapped" by the madman's plot are singing "Row, Row, Row Your Boat." It's the same song that the kids trapped by the madman in Dirty Harry are forced to sing.

Anthony Peck, who plays Ricky Walsh was also in the original Die Hard. He is credited as "Young Cop".

During its Pay Per View run in 1996, a bonus featurette followed the presentation of the movie which included footage of some scenes with additional dialogue such as the scene in the Federal Reserve Bank where Felix Little asks "You're in the flower business, Mr. Vanderflug?" and added is Simon replying "It's Vanderfluge, it rhymes with tulip." explaining why Felix pronounces the name correctly from that point on. This featurette is not included in the Special Edition DVD.

The film was shot under the working title "Die Hard: New York."

The main theme for this movie is "When Johnny comes Marching Home," an Irish song made famous in America by Patrick Sarsfield Gilmore aka Louis Lambert in 1863.

In the wake of the Oklahoma bombing, 20th Century Fox took out trade press ads defending their decision to continue with the imminent release of a film about a terrorist planting bombs in public places.

The bridge from which McClane and Zeus jump to the container ship in the harbor is the Cooper River Bridge that connects Charleston and Mount Pleasant, South Carolina. A new bridge opened in July 2005, and the two pre-existing bridges that have long been a symbol of Charleston will be removed. Much of the film was shot in the Charleston area, including the subway station which was built on a stage in Mount Pleasant. The Cooper River Bridge scenes were set on an unnamed bridge near Bridgeport, CT, on Long Island Sound.

WILHELM SCREAM: As they are driving through the park Zeus asks McClane if he is aiming for the people, to which McClane replies, "No... maybe that mime." An abbreviated Wilhelm Scream can be heard immediately following the "No."

First version of the screenplay was based on a spec script by James Haggin called "Troubleshooter" which involved terrorists seizing control of a Caribbean cruise ship. The idea was abandoned after Under Siege (1992) went into production. In 1992 John Milius was hired to write another version of the story. In 1993 Doug Richardson and John Fasano simultaneously worked on two separate Die Hard 3 scripts which were both rejected by Bruce Willis. This time the plot was concerned with terrorists taking control of the L.A. subway system.

Character "Dr. Fred Schiller" is a reference to the 18th century German poet Friedrich Schiller, who wrote the lyrics used by Ludwig van Beethoven in his 9th symphony, which is used in Die Hard (1988).

The name Simon Gruber uses as an alias is 'Peter Krieg'. 'Krieg' is German for 'war'.

Even though this film's domestic box office is only about 100 million dollars, its massive international box office (which is about 266 million dollars) makes this film the "highest worldwide box office winner of 1995". This movie is perhaps one of the few movies (may be the only one) that could manage to become the "biggest worldwide box office winner of the year" when its domestic box office was not even in the top 5.

There is a war reference in each of the first three Die Hard films. This film's is when the FBI agent references the Battle of the Bulge.

The original casting of Simon's terrorist crew was with a mix of Soviet and Warsaw Pact baddies and not East Germans. Only one Polish character (Otto) was retained from initial casting and he became the butt of the East German's demeaning jokes.

An early script that was rejected was eventually used for Speed 2: Cruise Control (1997). On the DVD commentary director John McTiernan mentions the rejected idea of "doing it on a boat."

There is a mathematical formula that can be applied to the St. Ives problem, called the Geometric Progression Formula, which is $a(r^n - 1)/(r-1)$, "a" being the first term, "r" being the common ratio, and "n" being the number of terms of the geometric series. The 7 wives would be "a". The following 7s would be the common ratio. "N" would be 4 (i.e. kittens, cats, sacks, and wives). This translates to $7(7^4 - 1)/(7-1) = 7(2401-1)/6 = 7(2400)/6 = 16800/6 = 2800$. This is all assuming the narrator going to St. Ives. and the man with seven wives are excluded.

Jeremy Irons replaced David Thewlis as Simon.

When Simon, posing as the city engineer, meets Ricky Walsh, you can see a blurry but visible red sign on the building in the background. This is the Home Insurance Company building and that company purchased the red cover so that it would be seen in the movie as they felt that the original bronze signage would not be visible.

Danny Cannon was approached to direct but he was more interested in making Judge Dredd (1995) at the time.

The first Die Hard to not occur on Christmas, though the holiday is referenced by John McClane and Simon Gruber.

The dump truck driven by John McClane has "Thur & Samson Earth Movers, Inc." on the door. The locations department for the movie include a Pamela Thur and Robin F. Samson.

In real life, Alan Rickman is more than 2 and a half years older than Jeremy Irons, despite the fact that in the 'Die Hard' film series, Irons plays the older brother.

On the DVD commentary Director John McTiernan mentions that Dick Cheney appears in a scene. He actually says "here he is", but Dick Cheney is not in the film - the person shown in the scene has a slight physical resemblance but is not Dick Cheney. The director made an error.

Each of the first 3 'Die Hard' films has a connection and/or reference to at least 1 of the 3 countries of Northern Europe: Norway, Sweden, and Finland. Here, in the third one, it is during the scene when Walsh mentions Oslo, and Cobb asks, "Norway?".

Aldis Hodge and his brother Edwin, made their acting debuts in this film. And Aldis would later appear in another " Die Hard" film eighteen years later as a different character named 'Foxy' in "A Good Day to Die Hard".

While the highway scenes are supposed to take place on the Saw Mill Parkway in Westchester County, NY, they were actually filmed on the Merritt Parkway in Fairfield County, Connecticut, and on the Taconic Parkway in Putnam County, NY.

Known screenwriter Michael Cristofer, who plays agent Bill Jarvis in this movie, wrote The Bonfire of the Vanities (1990), which also starred Bruce Willis in another story that takes place in New York.

Film debut of Kevin Chamberlin.

The truck driver who helps John McLain navigate through the aquaduct can be seen in the angry crowd of parents outside of the school with the suspected bomb in it.

Simon Gruber's phone number is 555-0001.

Despite not being set at Christmas, it still references Die Hard (1988) and Die Hard 2 (1990) (which were set at Christmas) with sarcastic comments regarding Santa Claus. The shoplifting kids also say "It's Christmas, you could steal city hall!" While in the aqueduct, McClane further mentions "We got a report of some guy coming through here with eight reindeer", then shoots the terrorist and continues, "They said he was a jolly old fat guy, with a snowy white beard, and a cute little red-and-white suit. I'm surprised you guys didn't see him."

McClane only has two bullets at his disposal to kill Simon in the finale of the film. He also only had two bullets in the first Die Hard to kill Simon's brother, Hans, and his last remaining associate.

There are two solutions to the water jug riddle in the park, at the elephant fountain. To place exactly 4 gallons of water on the scales when you only have two jugs which hold 3 and 5 gallons respectively, you must do either of the following. 1. Fill the 5 gallon jug and decant the water into the 3 gallon jug. This leaves two gallons in the big jug. 2. Empty the 3 gallon jug and pour in the two gallons from the 5 gallon jug, leaving space for one gallon in the small jug. 3. Refill the 5 gallon jug and pour water from it into the 3 gallon jug until the small jug's full. 4. That leaves exactly four gallons in the big jug; put it on the scale and the bomb is disarmed. The second method is: 1. Fill the 3 gallon jug and pour the water into the 5 gallon jug. 2. Refill the 3 gallon jug, and pour into the 5 gallon jug until the big jug is full, leaving one gallon in the small jug. 3. Empty the big jug, and transfer the one gallon from the small jug to the big jug. 4. Refill the small jug and pour all three gallons into the 5 gallon jug, resulting in four gallons in the big jug. Place the big jug on the scale and the bomb is disarmed.

Each of the Gruber brothers, Simon and Hans, recruit a Karl on his team. Karl in Die Hard (1988) is the terrorist shot by Sgt. Powell at the end. In this film Karl is stationed at the Federal Reserve bank and is killed by McClane in the elevator sequence.

When posing as a city engineer, Simon Gruber (Jeremy Irons) uses a heavy American accent to fool his adversaries. The same trick was used by his brother Hans (Alan Rickman) in Die Hard (1988).

The 2003 R1 DVD version includes the original ending showing McClane and Simon playing a game of 'chicken' with a rocket launcher. In this original version, Simon Gruber and his crew get away with the gold and months later, McClane tracks Simon down in Eastern Europe (where in Europe is debated: McClane mentions Germany, but people in the background are heard speaking Hungarian) The number on the bottom of the aspirin bottle (at the phone booth) leads McClane to Gruber. The gold was turned into small miniatures of the Empire State building and smuggled out of the country. McClane is thrown off the force, with the police thinking that he may actually be involved in the heist. The "game" that McClane and Simon play is about riddles that McClane tells Simon, and he is supposed to figure out the answer, or McClane will force him to fire a rocket launcher with its directional arrows removed, so neither will know which direction it will fire in until it is actually fired. The scene climaxes with McClane forcing Simon at gunpoint to fire the rocket launcher, which kills Simon, and McClane is revealed to be wearing a flak-jacket, which would have saved his life if the rocket launcher had fired at him instead of Simon. The studio objected to the ending, saying that it made McClane too cruel and heartless, whereas screenwriter Jonathan Hensleigh stated that that was exactly the point: to show that McClane had been pushed over the edge by the events of that day, and then subsequently losing everything as a result of Simon.

The final fight between McClane and Simon takes place at a truck stop in Quebec. The scenes were filmed at a truck stop off of I-95 in Jessup, Maryland.

Live Free or Die Hard (2007)
128 min - Action | Adventure | Thriller - 27 June
2007 (USA)

John McClane and a young hacker join forces to take
down master cyber-terrorist Thomas Gabriel in
Washington D.C.

Director: Len Wiseman
Writers: Mark Bomback (screenplay), Mark Bomback
(story),
Stars: Bruce Willis, Justin Long, Timothy Olyphant

-A Couple Of Average Joe's
Live Free or Die Hard is the 4th movie in the Die Hard
franchise and the first one that was rated PG-13. That
rating killed the movie, taking out all the
conventional "Die Hard-isms" that make these movies
"Die Hard" movies. There are certain expectations
when it comes to these movies, Bruce Willis wise
cracking to the bad guys, explosions and Yippee Ki Yay
mother fucker. Creating these movies is a simple
process, John McClane finds himself in a situation that
requires him to beat on bad guys until he's a mess and
they are dead. That being said, the action scenes are
top notch and the movie IS fun, but the unrated DVD
version is even better. It's a shame when the studios
get involved and screw things up for a movie that you
almost can't screw up.

John McClane doesn't kill a bad guy until over an hour into this movie. That is longer than any Die Hard movie.

It took four months to assemble and combine archive footage of past American presidents from Franklin D. Roosevelt to George W. Bush to create the televised warning from Gabriel. The goal was to create a video representation of a ransom note.

In the elevator shaft scene where Mai Lihn swings on the wire and flies into the truck and hits McClane, the stunt double accidentally cut Bruce Willis' eyebrow with her spiked heel and according to Len Wiseman in the DVD Commentary, she jabbed Willis hard enough that when medics examined the injury, the brow bone was exposed.

Bruce Willis' stunt double, Larry Rippenkroeger, was seriously injured when he fell 25 feet to the pavement. He suffered broken bones in his face and fractures in both wrists. Production was temporarily shut down. Willis picked up the tab at area hotels for Larry's parents and visited him a number of times at the hospital. Larry also doubles for James Caan in his TV series, Las Vegas (2003). Caan came and visited Larry in the hospital and joked around for over an hour. Larry told his parents he was glad when Caan left because he hurt so bad laughing at Caan's jokes.

The stunt featuring McClane driving a police car into a helicopter took three weeks to rehearse. The shot was accomplished by suspending the helicopter in the air with cables and combining two separate shots; one of the stuntman leaping from the helicopter and one of the car colliding with it. Computer animation was then used to delete the support cables and add rotor blades.

Kevin Smith rewrote the lines for his Warlock character. Bruce Willis thought the rewrite was too funny and did not follow the serious mood of the movie. Smith then rewrote the part to what Willis requested.

According to Bruce Willis and Director Len Wiseman in the DVD Commentary, the story originally involved McClane's son, Jack. Originally, he was supposed to be the computer hacker John has to deliver to the FBI. Eventually that idea was dropped and the hacker became the Matt Farrell character. It was then decided to bring in his daughter Lucy to keep up the series theme of McClane always having a personal stake in what happens in the story.

When McClane is driving toward the helicopter, he says, "You think a traffic jam, throwing a car at me is gonna stop me, huh?" Director Len Wiseman dubbed the last part of this line ("Gonna stop me"), imitating the voice of Bruce Willis.

French actor and martial artist Cyril Raffaelli, who plays Rand, does his stunts almost without special effects and wires.

The first Die Hard film where no reference is made to Christmas.

The only Die Hard movie to take place over the course of more than one day.

This film addresses the apparent continuity error in earlier installments - McClane is afraid of flying in Die Hard (1988) and Die Hard 2 (1990), but not Die Hard: With a Vengeance (1995). Here, he explains that he took flying lessons in order to "face his fears."

The phrase "Live free or die" is from a toast written by the revolutionary soldier General John Stark. The full phrase is "Live free or die: Death is not the worst of evils".

In the beginning credits when Kevin Smith's name comes on the screen. The "m" in smith disappears and you see "Sith" for a few seconds paying homage to Kevin Smith's love of all things Star Wars which also reflects in his character in the movie.

The first sequel in the series where no character mentions John McClane's encounter at the Nakatomi Plaza in L.A. in Die Hard (1988). However, visual references to Nakatomi Plaza are seen while Thomas Gabriel is looking at John McClane's dossier.

In addition to the 'Agent Johnson' reference, several other elements from the first Die Hard (1988) film are revisited as series trademarks. Among them are: crawling on broken glass, use of air-ducts, elevator shafts, and maintenance areas in corporate buildings, a henchman falling down stairs, an inquiry on the E.T.A. of a helicopter, and McClane's "Yippie Ki Yay' catchphrase.

The plot point of McClane having to rescue a kidnapped Lucy was carried over from a rejected script for Die Hard: With a Vengeance (1995).

The bad guy Thomas Gabriel points a gun at McClane and declares "On your tombstone it will say 'Always in the wrong place at the wrong time'." "John McClane is back in the wrong place at the wrong time!" was a tagline used for Die Hard 2 (1990).

When released on DVD on 20th November, 2007 in the US and Canada, it became the first DVD ever to be packaged with a Digital Copy.

A water treatment facility near Los Angeles doubled as the film's Woodlawn Social Security Administration building. The facility has miles of underground tunnels, and was also used in Die Hard 2 (1990) when Bruce Willis runs through tunnels under the airport.

The first film in the series where the antagonist does not use a fake accent. In Die Hard (1988), Hans Gruber faked an American accent to fool McClane; in Die Hard 2 (1990), Colonel Stuart fakes a Midwestern accent while guiding an airline pilot into crashing into the ground; and in Die Hard: With a Vengeance (1995), Simon fakes an American accent while posing as a city engineer.

When filming the scenes of John walking through the corridors talking to Gabriel on the two-way, there were no written lines of dialog for Bruce Willis, according to Len Wiseman on the DVD Commentary. So what they did on set was have Willis hold the two-way up to his mouth and speak gibberish so it looks like he's talking to Gabriel. If you'll notice, there are a couple of times where the two-way isn't all the way up to Willis's face and you can see his mouth doesn't match the dialog being spoken.

The elevator shaft sequence was not in the film's script when Len Wiseman was hired as director. Wiseman added it because he associated elevator shafts and claustrophobic spaces with Die Hard (1988).

Scott Speedman was Len Wiseman's first choice for the role of Matt Farrell whereas Ben Affleck was Bruce Willis' first choice for the role. Willis wanted Affleck in order to recreate the chemistry between two characters previously accomplished in Armageddon (1998)

The Terminator action figure in Matt's apartment is a nod to executive producer William Wisher Jr. and composer Marco Beltrami. Wisher co-wrote and appeared in The Terminator (1984) and Terminator 2: Judgment Day (1991), and Beltrami composed the score for Terminator 3: Rise of the Machines (2003).

When Gabriel is talking to McClane over the phone and pulling up his information on the computer, Bonnie Bedelia makes a cameo appearance in the form of her character Holly McClane's driver's license photo. The photo appears as though it may be either a publicity shot from a prior "Die Hard" film or a still photo (i.e. family portrait) from one of the movies.

When McClane throws Russo down the stairs, the stuntman landed so hard that his impact dented one of the thick metal steps.

This is the first Die Hard film without the music of film composer Michael Kamen. Kamen died in 2003. Portions of Kamen's previous "Die Hard" scores, however, were incorporated into the score by Marco Beltrami.

The film was edited down to a PG-13 rating for commercial reasons, thus making it the first film in the series not rated R. The DVD version is unrated and restores much of the profanity and violence that was trimmed for this purpose, making the film an equivalent of an R rating.

John McClane's date of birth is revealed as May 23, 1955 when Thomas Gabriel looks at his dossier.

The only Die Hard film that is set in multiple states (New Jersey, Washington DC, West Virginia, and Baltimore). The other three Die Hard films were all set in and around (or above) primarily one location throughout most of the movies.

All the IP-addresses shown in the movie are legal ones. However, most start with either 10, 172.16 or 192.168. Those numbers are reserved for local traffic only. At 02:04, one of the hackers transfers data with scp to 202.218.154.52, which is owned by a Japanese company.

The name "Tovarek", which Mai Lihn uses as an FBI agent, is a Polish word and one of its meanings is "hot chick" (the correct Polish word is "towarek", but it's pronounced like this). Tara Tovarek is also the name of producer Michael Fottrell's assistant.

Justin Timberlake was in talks to play John McClane's son.

A single frame shot of director Len Wiseman's wife Kate Beckinsale is spliced into the opening credits, when the van is outside the exploding house.

The movie's title, "Live Free or Die Hard", is a reference to New Hampshire's State Motto "Live Free or Die". Consequently, the New Hampshire state film office received several phone calls asking where in the state the movie was filmed.

In the beginning of the film, John McClane and Lucy have an argument that eventually leads to them discussing her use of her mother's last name, "Gennero". A similar argument takes place in Die Hard (1988), when McClane is searching for the location of his wife, Holly, in the Nakatomi building. He does not find her under "McClane," but does find her under her maiden name "Gennaro", which is misspelled.

On the DVD commentary, director Len Wiseman discusses the "back yard Die Hard (1988)" he shot when he was younger. At least one of the shots from it was used in this film, and Wiseman acted it out for Bruce Willis during filming so that Willis could duplicate it.

The opening scene between McClane and Lucy was filmed on the campus of the University of Southern California in Los Angeles. The building that serves as Lucy's dormitory is actually Doheny Library.

This is the only installment of the series where John McClane doesn't carry his Beretta 92FS. Instead he carries either a SIG-Sauer P220R.

The first film in the Die Hard series not to be shot in the anamorphic Panavision process. This film was shot in Super 35 to save money with visual effects.

When McClane is driving in Jersey and talking to the chief captain of Camden, the guy's name is Wiseman, same name as the director, Len Wiseman, although pronounced 'Wheezeman', as this was how most crew-members thought his name should be pronounced. The voice is that of the director himself.

The car that is stolen in the film by McClane and Farrell is a 2006 E60 BMW 5 series, which was chosen due to a poll that found that people wanted films that had more BMWs in it. The main reason given was that the alternatives (Audis and Mercedes-Benzes) were too common and not bold and imposing enough to go with the characters in the film. The particular BMW model (5 series) was chosen because the director, Len Wiseman, found "the 3 series too common, the 7 series too uptight and every other car either too feminine or compensating for a midlife crisis... Everything McClane isn't, yet".

The script was not originally written to be a 'Die Hard' sequel.

While in early development with a script that was eventually discarded, the movie had been given the subtitle "Tears of the Sun". Bruce Willis told the studio he would commit to a Die Hard 4 if he could use the title for Tears of the Sun (2003).

Jessica Simpson auditioned unsuccessfully for the role of Bruce Willis' daughter. She can be seen going to and then coming from the audition in Newlyweds: Nick & Jessica: Mismatched Threesome (2004).

So far, this is the only film that Len Wiseman directed that didn't star Kate Beckinsale or Bill Nighy.

The French title translates as "Die Hard 4.0: Return to Hell".

Prints were sent out to UK cinemas under the fake name "New Hampshire" - a reference to the state's "Live Free or Die" motto and the movie's original title - in spite of the title being changed to "Die Hard 4.0" in European territories.

William Wisher Jr., co-writer of The Terminator (1984) and Terminator 2: Judgment Day (1991), made uncredited contributions to the script.

The screen to the far left of all of Warlock's hacking screens has the auction website eBay open with a Boba Fett action figure being watched, despite the fact that the power had already been cut off by that time in the screenplay.

The filming title used by the crew and to mark locations was "Reset".

Britney Spears and Taylor Fry auditioned for the role of Lucy McClane.

According to the files that Thomas Gabriel pull up on Holly Gennero, her Driver License records list her address as the fictitious 9975 Geyser Way East, San Francisco, CA, 9424- (the smaller picture on her license obscures the final ZIP code digit).

Kal Penn and Brad Renfro both auditioned for the role of Matt before it went to Justin Long.

Tony Jaa was rumored for a role in the film.

Rob Huebel auditioned for the role of Matt Farrell.

Director Cameo
Len Wiseman: Pilot of the F35 jet.

Director Len Wiseman credits actor Timothy Olyphant (Thomas Gabriel) with coming up with the idea of how McClane kills Gabriel. In order to keep it a secret, the scene was not included in the film's shooting script.

The film's climax originally involved McClane racing alongside an exploding gas pipeline on a motorcycle with Matt in a sidecar. The idea evolved into Gabriel trying to kill McClane and Matt by routing gas to their location through the pipelines.

Live Free or Die Hard (2007) was retro-fitted from the original screenplay WW3.com, which was nearly filmed on its own merits before the 9/11 terrorist attacks caused it to be shelved.

Bruce Willis has openly stated he would like to bring back Bonnie Bedelia to the franchise. She originally played the character of Holly Gennaro McClane, the wife of Bruce Willis' character John McClane in Die Hard (1988) and Die Hard 2 (1990) in the film franchise. Her character hasn't been utilized in the franchise since.

A Good Day to Die Hard (2013)
98 min - Action | Crime | Thriller - 14 February
2013 (USA)

John McClane travels to Russia to help out his
seemingly wayward son, Jack, only to discover that Jack
is a CIA operative working undercover, causing the
father and son to team up against underworld forces.

Director: John Moore
Writers: Skip Woods, Roderick Thorp (certain original
characters by)
Stars: Bruce Willis, Jai Courtney, Sebastian Koch

-A Couple Of Average Joe's
John Moore's contribution to the Die Hard series seems
to be just phoning it in. McClane ends up in Russia to
help Jack out, only to find out that Jack is an
undercover agent and that his cover has been blown
thanks to his dad! Damn you father McClane! This movie
seems to ape both Die Hard With A Vengeance and Live
Free or Die Hard, but it doesn't take the best of those
movies, it merely just copies the moments and they
become mediocre at best. Some of the action scenes were
really well done, but the interplay between Jack and
John was forced and wooden. The basics are still there,
the bad guys stealing money, explosions, helicopters
firing into buildings and McClane getting beat up. In
the end, you're better off throwing on Die Hard and re-
watching that.

Bruce Willis is the only cast or crew member involved
in all five Die Hard (1988) films.

The largest helicopter in the film is a Mil Mi-26 (NATO
reporting name: Halo). It is also the largest and the
most powerful helicopter ever produced.

The Russian gang had no actual Russian members. The
roles were played by Slovakian, Hungarian, Serbian,
Mongolian and Ukrainian actors.

This is the first Die Hard (1988) sequel since Die Hard
2 (1990) where a performer (besides Bruce Willis) has
reprised a role as a cameo. Mary Elizabeth Winstead
reprises her role of Lucy McClane from Live Free or Die

Hard (2007). Besides Winstead and Willis, the only other actors to appear more than once in the "Die Hard" films are Reginald VelJohnson, William Atherton, and Bonnie Bedelia (who all appeared in the first two entries), Anthony Peck who played a young cop in the first and Ricky Walsh in the third film and Aldis Hodge who played Zeus' nephew Raymond in Die Hard: With a Vengeance (1995), and CIAgent Foxy in this film (wearing military fatigues and telling Jack his window for extraction is lost).

Aaron Paul, Liam Hemsworth, James Badge Dale, Paul Walker, Ben Foster, Shiloh Fernandez, Milo Ventimiglia, Paul Dano, Steven R. McQueen, and D.J. Cotrona were considered to play John McClane's son. The role ultimately was earned by Jai Courtney.

Filming of the Mi-24 Hind helicopter firing scenes took place at a military shooting range where Major Peter Simon, Air Operations Commander of Szolnok Helicopter Base, Hungarian Air Force (the pilot of the helicopter in all scenes) operated the gunship's Gryazev-Shipunov GS-30-2k (30 mm) auto-cannons and S-8 (80 mm) rockets with live ammunition to make sure the shooting effects will be as realistic as possible. Background and targets were applied in post-production.

The city of Pripyat was founded in 1970 for workers at the nearby Chernobyl nuclear power plant.

The black Mercedes SUV featured in a chase scene is a Mercedes-Benz G-Class. The line was developed after the Shah of Iran suggested it to the Daimler-Benz management as a possible military vehicle. Shah Mohammad Reza Pahlavi was a major Daimler shareholder at the time.

In the UK, digital copies of the film were delivered to cinemas with the fake title "Simon Says", a tagline from the third installment, Die Hard: With a Vengeance (1995).

The Mil Mi-26 transport helicopter seen at the end of the movie was rented from the Ministry of Emergency Situations of the Republic of Belarus. The original color of the helicopter is white. The temporary camouflage paint scheme was applied in Hungary, where the helicopter scenes were shot.

Uranium-235 is a rare isotope of Uranium-238, with atoms that contain the same number of protons but fewer neutrons. "Weapons grade Uranium" is refined Uranium-235 containing less than 15% Uranium-238.

The Cougar HEV armored truck was portrayed by four replica vehicles: three custom vehicles made by the specialists of Team Szalay, built on chassis of military surplus 6-wheeled ZIL 131 trucks, and powered by Ural truck engines. The fourth replica used for jump stunts was made in the US and was powered by a V10 Dodge Viper engine.

The McClanes steal a Maybach 57. Maybach is Daimler AG's premium marque, but it is operating at a loss. Daimler will cease Maybach production in 2013.

At 97 minutes, this is the shortest film in the series since Die Hard 2 (1990): Die Harder.

In the final action scene, the helicopter pilot says that the controls are at "full forward cyclic." This means that the cyclic stick (the joystick-like control) is pushed all the way forward in an attempt to bring the nose down.

The first Die Hard film to be released in the IMAX format.

This is Aldis Hodge's second appearance in the Die Hard series. His first appearance was in Die Hard: With a Vengeance (1995), where he played Zeus' oldest nephew.

Noam Murro was originally the director, but his commitment to the film 300: Rise of an Empire (2014) prevented him from working on this film. Other directors considered including Joe Cornish, Justin Lin and Nicolas Winding Refn.

The first Die Hard film to be shown in the 1.85:1 aspect ratio, as well as the first to be shot on Fuji film stock.

Murphy, played by Amaury Nolasco refers to McClane as 'papi', which is a term that Nolasco's character of Sucre often used in Prison Break (2005).

The 6-wheeled Force Protection Cougar HEV truck used in the street chase and car destruction scenes was driven by Zolee Ganxsta (real name: Zoltán Zana), a well-known Hungarian rapper and drummer, also famous for his extensive tattoos, playing a Russian gangster.

Jai Courtney and Robert Patrick share the distinction of appearing in the Die Hard franchise and the Terminator franchise. Jai Courtney appears as Jack McClane in A Good Day to Die Hard (2013) and as Kyle Reese in Terminator Genisys (2015). Robert Patrick appears in Die Hard 2 (1990) as a henchman and in Terminator 2: Judgment Day (1991) as T-1000, a main character.

Shot with Super 35, and with the series' traditional 2.35:1 scope aspect ratio in mind, director John Moore re-framed the film to 1.85:1 (possible through the Super 35 format) after deciding the opening car chase sequence looked better that way. He also believed the 1.85:1 ratio would better accommodate the hand-held camera work scenes.

John McClane's cellphone ringtone, is Ludwig van Beethoven's Ode to Joy, a theme song of the first Die Hard (1988) film.

Eric Jacobus and his stunt team designed (and filmed a screen test) of a fight scene between Bruce Willis and Radivoje Bukvic. The scene would have featured Alik attacking John McClane with a knife on a rooftop, but their choreography was not utilized.

The private jet seen at the end of the film is a Hawker 400XP.

The first film produced by TSG Entertainment.

When Chagarin visits Komorov in the prison, Komorov plays a white chess piece before flipping to the black chess side of the board. This of course hints his duality later in the film.

This is the first "Die Hard" film where Bruce Willis' character does not kill the main antagonist.

Becomes the 4th out of the 5 films to feature an exploding helicopter, but if you count the planes from Die Hard 2 (1990), then all five films have had an aircraft explode in mid air.

The Fog (1980)

The centenary of the small seaside town of Antonio Bay,
California is approaching. One hundred years ago, the
wealthy leper Blake bought the clipper ship Elizabeth
Dane and sailed with his people to form a leper colony.

Director: John Carpenter
Writers: John Carpenter, Debra Hill
Stars: Adrienne Barbeau, Jamie Lee Curtis, Janet Leigh
|

John Carpenter's ghost story does more right than wrong
by taking the "less is more approach" and maintaining
its creepiness throughout. The foil is set right at
the beginning with John Houseman's engrossing campfire
tale. Each attack by the vengeful ghost harkens back
to those scary moments as a kid hiding under the
covers. As with Halloween, Carpenter's score adds to
the scare factor. Jamie Lee Curtis as a loose
hitchhiker doesn't get much to say but, at least
Adrienne Barbeau takes the lead and does well with it.
You'll never look at wood washing up on the shore the
same way again.

After a rough cut editing the movie appeared to be much
too short for a theatrical release (about 80 minutes),
John Carpenter subsequently added the prologue with the
Old Captain telling ghost stories to fascinated
children by a campfire.

Bennett, Father Malone's assistant at the beginning of
the film, was played by John Carpenter but was
uncredited.

The Fog was shot in thirty days.

Blake, the lead ghost, was played by makeup specialist
Rob Bottin. When Bottin asked for the job, John
Carpenter asked him to "stand up". Bottin then expected
Carpenter to say, "...and get out!" When Carpenter saw
that Bottin was a very large man, which was needed for
the Blake character, he was hired.

While driving to the lighthouse, Stevie flips around the radio dial, and a broadcast confirming a search for the ship The Sea Grass is heard. The voice mentions "a sweep south of Waitely Point and Arkham Reef". Both Arkham Reef and the surname "Waitely" are references to writer H.P. Lovecraft, as he used both repeatedly in his stories.

Carpenter is an admitted Lovecraft fan.

Although this was essentially a low budget independent film, John Carpenter chose to shoot the movie in anamorphic widescreen Panavision. This decision gave the film a grander feel for the viewer so it didn't seem like a low budget horror film.

Adrienne Barbeau patterned her voice after a female disc jockey from the 1960's known as the Night Bird.

The film's opening prologue was a quote from the final two lines of Edgar Allan Poe's poem "A Dream Within a Dream". It states: "Is all that we see or seem but a dream withing a dream".

John Houseman's opening monologue, which is supposed to transpire over a course of five minutes (from 11:55 to 12:00 midnight) is, in fact, only 2 minutes and 25 seconds long from the moment he mentions it is 11:55 to the moment the bells ring in the background, signaling midnight. It has been incorrectly noted in the past that this opening monologue is exactly five minutes long.

Actresses Janet Leigh and Jamie Lee Curtis are in real-life mother and daughter respectively.

As Stevie calls out the progress of the fog through town over the radio, she mentions Russelville road and Smallhouse road. These are two prominent streets in Bowling Green, Kentucky, where John Carpenter spent time growing up.

Adrienne Barbeau and Jamie Lee Curtis, the leads, do not appear together in any scenes.

The band mentioned on the radio near the beginning is "The Coupe DeVilles", which features director John Carpenter.

John Carpenter has stated two inspirations for the film, both of which are related to Great Britain. The first was the British film The Crawling Eye (1958) which dealt with monsters hiding in the clouds. He also stated that he and his co-writer/producer, Debra Hill, were inspired by a trip to Stonehenge, the ancient monument in South West England, which was covered in fog during their visit.

Actress Adrienne Barbeau and director John Carpenter were married at the time the film was made and released.

The role of Father Malone was originally offered to Christopher Lee who believed the character to be the 'father of the community'. However Lee proved unavailable and Hal Holbrook was eventually cast.

Dr. Phibes, the name of the coroner played by Darwin Joston, is an in-joke reference to Dr. Anton Phibes, the character played by Vincent Price in the horror film The Abominable Dr. Phibes (1971) and its sequel Dr. Phibes Rises Again (1972).

Jazz music was used for Stevie Wayne's radio station because it was more affordable than rock music.

The journal's last page that Father Malone (Hal Holbrook) read when he finds it in the wall says: "April 30 - Midnight 'til one belong to the dead. Good Lord deliver us". It's a reference for Walpurgis Night, a pagan feast which happens in the night between April 30 and May 1.

The sword that Blake carries is a Pattern 1796 Light Cavalry Sabre with an iron scabbard, produced between 1796 and 1821. Designed by Brigade Major John Le Marchant and Birmingham sword cutler Henry Osborn.

The quote "like an albatross around the neck" can be heard on the record cassette in the lighthouse where Stevie Wayne (Adrienne Barbeau) works, just before that a wooden piece with the word "Dane" explodes when the quote "6 Must Die" appears magically written in it. The quote about the albatross belongs to The Rime of the Ancient Mariner, created by Samuel Taylor Coleridge and published in 1798.

Kurt Russell was offered a role.

Probably no coincidence given Carpenter's penchant for subtle references that the vehicle seen Stevie Wayne character driving with the radio call sign "KAB" on the side is a Volkswagen "Thing" - a vehicle Volkswagenproduced from 1968 to 1983 (also known as a Type 181. but marketed in the U.S. under the "Thing" name.

The name of the old antique grandfather's diary found inside the wall of the church was the "Journal of Father Patrick Malone 1880".

First of two ghost story horror pictures that veteran actor John Houseman made in a two year period. The second film was Universal Pictures' Ghost Story (1981). The two roles were similar parts.

The name of the old clipper ship was the "Elizabeth Dane" whilst the names of other boats seen in the picture were "Hyperio" the "Lady Laura" and partially obscured, but most-telling "Halloween."

The name of the radio station was KAB Radio 1340.

Creepshow (1982)
120 min - Comedy | Horror - 12 November 1982 (USA)

Inspired by the E.C. comics of the 1950s, George
A.Romero and Stephen King bring five tales of terror to
the screen.

Director: George A. Romero
Writer: Stephen King (screenplay)
Stars: Hal Holbrook, Leslie Nielsen, Adrienne Barbeau

Creepshow was one of those vignette style movies that
took five different stories and tied them all together
by using a guide of sorts to move the viewer from tale
to tale. Each one of the stories in Creepshow is about
people getting what they deserved and George Romero
does a masterful job of pulling all of the stories
together, as disparate as each story is from the next
Romero is able to do what a lot of filmmakers aren't
able to do and that is to take five stories and turn
them into a movie that the viewer can follow with out
getting lost. Very few directors can scare the hell out
of you like Romero can and it's nice to see the master
of the zombie genre take on different styles with
Creepshow.

In every episode of Creepshow there is a hidden little
glass horse.

"the Lonesome Death Of Jordy Verrill was based on the
Stephen King Short titled "Weeds".

Other movies Leslie Nielson starred in Airplane!
Airplane II!, the Naked Gun movies.

The boy who is the collector of Creepshow Comics? Joe
King, Stephen's son.

Tom Savini the makeup effects artist is also one of the
garbage men during the between the stories scenes.

Gaylen Ross, Leslie Nielson's wife in the movie was one
of the stars of Dawn of the Dead.

George Romero's wife has a cameo in the short "The Crate" .

The ashtray from the first story appears in all 5 shorts.

The wrestling match Jordy Verrill is watching showed then WWF Champion Bob Backlund and the Samoan No. 1.

Rice Krispies were used as maggots on the corpse's eyes in the first story "Father's Day".

A sign leading to Castle Rock appears at the very end of Jordy Verrill's story.

The film playing in the background of the Jordy Verrill short was "how Green Was My Valley.

The monster in "The Crate" was named Fluffy by George Romero.

Creepshow 2 was banned in Sweden.

Stephen King appears in "The Hitchhiker" as a truck driver.

The raft is adapted from a Stephen King short story from the book Skeleton Crew.

Tom Savini plays the Creep at the beginning and end of the Creepshow 2.

Page Hannah, who plays Rachel in "The Raft" is the sister of Daryl Hannah.

There were supposed to be 5 stories for Creepshow 2 but two of them were scrapped because of budget. The 2 stories? Pinfall and Cat From Hell. Cat From Hell was filmed for Tales From The darkside The movie,

Tales from the Crypt (1989 - 1996)
TV Series - 25 min - Comedy | Crime | Horror

Tales of horror based on the gruesome EC horror comics
of the 1950's.

Stars: John Kassir, Roy Brocksmith, Miguel Ferrer

Appropriately placed on HBO as an R-rated type series,
this show got to express itselff in ways that network
televison was too scared to touch. Comically
represented by the necrotic Cryptkeeper, each tale was
as gory as it was uninhibited. For seven season of 93
episodes, this show had a large collection of
established actors and directors, unfortunately the
theatrical films weren't as well received and
successful. Worth a gander to see how uncensored
episodic television was down in the 90's. Unfortunately
the movies don't measure up to the television series,
but they're worth a look if you have the time.

There are 93 episodes of Tales From The Crypt.

John Kassir did the voice of "The Host", the
Cryptkeeper.

Kevin Yagher Designed The Cryptkeeper and Chucky, they
both have the same eyes, literally.

One Episode of the 93 wasn't from the Comics "The Third
Pig", it was the only animated episode.

Tales From The Crypt was originally conceived as a
trilogy, but turned into a TV series because of
concerns of box office performance.

3 movies did come out of the TV Series - Demon Knight,
Bordello Of Blood and Ritual.

Ritual was a straight to video release and was
disassociated with anything Tales From The Crypt until
2006.

The Cryptkeeper segments for the Ritual were reinserted
in 2006.

Tales from the Crypt started as an EC Comic in the 50's.

The Cryptkeeper has been spun off into 2 TV Shows 4 movies a radio show and a Christmas album.

The introduction sequence that started every episode through the Cryptkeeper's home is actually the size of a miniature golf course green. Small "snorkel" cameras were used to film this portion. The descent into the crypt in the end of the intro is computer generated.

John Kassir, voice of the Cryptkeeper, often had to swallow lemon juice and honey to sooth his throat after doing his lines.

The show was originally only planned for three seasons, but it proved so popular it lasted seven. Series creator William Gaines only lived to see season three.

It took six puppeteers to operate the Cryptkeeper during his scenes, four puppeteers alone just for his facial expressions.

While animatronics expert/puppetmaster Kevin Yagher was in the final stages of designing the Cryptkeeper, he tried on a few noses to see which would look best for the character - who had already shed lips, hair and most of his teeth - but none looked quite right. Director and producer Robert Zemeckis simply remarked, "You know, you don't necessarily have to have a nose."

For the episodes they directed, Walter Hill ("Cutting Cards") and Joel Silver ("Split Personality") studied the comic book originals they were based on and used them to plan out their shots.

Walter Hill cast William Sadler in the lead for "The Man Who Was Death" only if Sadler promised to perform exactly way he did for the audition.

The concept for the movie The Frighteners (1996) was originally going to be a TFTC film, but Robert Zemeckis loved the script so much that he had it spun off with Peter Jackson directing.

At William Gaines request, director Robert Zemeckis coaxed a bloodcurdling scream from Mary Ellen Trainor in the closing scene of "And All Through the House."

The series was released by HBO Home Video on 7 DVD Volumes in the USA and Canada. The series was released by HBO Home Video on 12 VHS Volumes in the USA and Canada.

Demon Knight was Purposely released on Friday, January 13 because the Tales From The Crypt movies were originally to be tied with traditional "horror weekends" such as Friday the 13th or Halloween.

Several concepts from demon knight, such as the idea of shooting demons in the eyes to send them back to Hell, was later used by writers Ethan Reiff and Cyrus Voris, for their television series Brimstone (1998).

In Demon Knight, Brayker says he received the key from a soldier named Dickerson, a reference to director Ernest R. Dickerson.

According to Corey Feldman, Dennis Miller was rude and disrespectful to the cast and crew. According to Feldman, Miller once stole a van from the transportation department and left the set. Feldman and Miller got into a heated confrontation during filming.

The key used in Bordello Of Blood is the same one used in Tales from the Crypt: Demon Knight (1995).

Bordello Of Blood was originally intended to be the second installment in a trilogy of Tales from the Crypt movies, but the proposed third movie was scrapped by Universal when Bordello of Blood bombed at the box offices.

In a cemetery, there's a crypt with the name "Gaines" on it. William Gaines is the creator of the "Tales from the Crypt" comic books.

Rafe (Dennis Miller) calls Vincent a demented Ewok. Phil Fondacaro, who plays Vincent, actually played an Ewok in Star Wars: Episode VI - Return of the Jedi (1983)

Whoopi Goldberg has a brief cameo in the movie.

The key used in the previous Crypt films, "Tales From The Crypt Presents: Demon Knight" and Bordello Of Blood is not used for the film Ritual.

This is Ron Taylor's last role as he passed away in 2002, shortly after appearing in this film.

Ritual is a remake of the 1943 film, I Walked With A Zombie.

The episode Lower Berth tells the Cryptkeepers origin his parents were a Mummy and a two-face man

Twilight Zone: The Movie (1983)
101 min - Horror | Sci-Fi - 24 June 1983 (USA)

Four horror/sci-fi segments directed by four famous
directors which are their own versions of classic
stories from Rod Serling's landmark television series.

Directors: Joe Dante, John Landis,
Writers: Rod Serling (television series The Twilight
Zone), John Landis (prologue),
Stars: Dan Aykroyd, Albert Brooks, Vic Morrow

Five stories reduced to four because of the on-set
tragedy. Borrowing from the original series classic
episodes, John Landis' film is drenched in the '80's.
John Lithgow seeing something on the wing of an
airplane is the films best segment though each tale has
something special. Vic Morrowas a tacists who gets the
tables turned on him is funny and insightful. Scatman
Crothers brings his personal charm to a convalescent
home and brings energy to a bunch of pre-death fuddy
duddies. Nancy Cartright (Bart Simpson) as Ethel is
just one of the frightened characters held hostage by a
"special" boy. Dan Akroyd's and Albert Brooks'
prolgogue scene sets the tone of the film by being
funny and scary simultaneously. A tad outdated, but
still a lot of fun.

On July 23, 1982, Vic Morrow, Renee Chen, and My-ca
Dinh Le, were killed on set when a helicopter crashed
on them during the filming of a Vietnam battle
sequence. Attorney James Neal defended John Landis -
who, along with George Folsey Jr., Dan Allingham, Paul
Stewart and Dorcey Wingo - was charged with involuntary
manslaughter. All were found not guilty.

According to John Larroquette, he requested to watch
the filming of what would become the tragic helicopter
scene, but his car was stolen the night before and he
was unable to get to the set.

In the opening title sequence, Rod Serling can be seen
in the reflection of the eye.

Another story considered by Steven Spielberg for the
film was one concerning a bully who has the tables

turned on him during Halloween night, but problems with the story ensued, and it was eventually scrapped.

William Shatner at one point was in consideration to reprise his lead role in the Nightmare at 20,000 Feet segment. He had to turn it down due to prior commitments. Ultimately John Lithgow was cast in the role.

Burgess Meredith, William Schallert, Kevin McCarthy, Bill Mumy, Murray Matheson and Patricia Barry all made guest appearances in Twilight Zone (1959). Furthermore, Schallert would later appear in the first revival series, The Twilight Zone (1985), while Mumy later appeared in the second, The Twilight Zone (2002).

Known for his meticulous preparation, John Lithgow had worked out certain scenes in his airplane seat in conjunction with the manufactured lightning outside the window. However, during filming, the crew member in charge of the lightning flashes would activate it too soon or too late, throwing off Lithgow's timing. Although initially annoyed, he later came to value the experience after viewing the film, seeing that it added to his anxious, fearful character as he looked genuinely startled by the lightning.

The name of Kathleen Quinlan's character is Helen Foley.

This was not the name of a character in the original "It's a Good Life" episode, but the name of a character from Twilight Zone: Nightmare as a Child (1960). Helen Foley was the name of one of Rod Serling's favorite teachers as a child.

In the diner, when Kathleen Quinlan is asked where she is from and where she is going, she answers with two town names that were used in old "Twilight Zone" episodes: "Homewood," from Twilight Zone: Walking Distance (1959), and "Willoughby," from Twilight Zone: A Stop at Willoughby (1960). The cook refers to "Cliffordville," from Twilight Zone: Of Late I Think of Cliffordville (1963).

Steven Spielberg briefly considered Rod Serling's Twilight Zone: The Monsters Are Due on Maple Street (1960) about neighborhood paranoia that's set off by a force of invading aliens from the original Twilight Zone series as a potential segment which he canceled because it involved nighttime filming with children and special effects. This was mainly due to the tragedy that occurred on the "Time Out" segment. He finally chose "Kick the Can" from the original series.

John Landis's segments were the first to be filmed, and Steven Spielberg considered canceling the entire project after the deadly helicopter crash. Ultimately the remaining segments were completed in this order: It's a Good Life, Nightmare at 20,000 Feet, and Kick the Can (Spielberg's segment).

The film originally started with Rod Serling's classic voiceover, but it was replaced with one by Burgess Meredith, who starred in four episodes of the original Twilight Zone series - Twilight Zone: Time Enough at Last (1959), Twilight Zone: Mr. Dingle, the Strong (1961), Twilight Zone: The Obsolete Man (1961), and Twilight Zone: Printer's Devil (1963).

Jerry Goldsmith's recording sessions for the score took place from February 28 to March 3, 1983, with each recording day devoted to each segment of the film. Steven Spielberg attended most of these sessions. However, it was Joe Dante who mainly supervised the entire session, filling in for George Miller and John Landis, who were not involved in the post-production of the film which included the music. Dante and Goldsmith would become good friends and begin a fruitful collaboration that would last over the next two decades (1983-2003).

The giant, glaring eye that Helen (Kathleen Quinlan) sees when she opens a door was used as part of the opening sequence for the series The Outer Limits (1995).

Frank Marshall, producer of the latter version, plays one of the ground crew members checking the plane's wing for damage.

The segments "It's a Good Life" and "Nightmare at 20,000 Feet" are both parodied in two Treehouse of Horror specials of The Simpsons (1989) (II & IV), and in both of them, Bart Simpson is the main character. Nancy Cartwright is the voice of Bart, and, she has a small role in this movie.

"Kick the Can," features Steven Spielberg's future mother-in-law, Priscilla Pointer, as Miss Cox.

The music for Segment 2 was originally written as the theme for Norman Bates in Psycho II (1983).

Exterior footage of the airplane on which John Valentine (John Lithgow) believes that he sees someone trying to sabotage the wing is of the Global Airways Boeing 707, from Skyjacked (1972) with added storm effects.

As of 2012, the Steven Spielberg segment of this movie is one of only two Spielberg-directed theatrical films not scored by John Williams; the other is The Color Purple (1985).

Mention is made of Lieutenant Neidermeyer getting "fragged" by his own troops. This was the fate given to Neidermeyer in the ending of Animal House (1978), also directed by John Landis.

When the time-traveling character Bill Connor finds himself targeted by the Ku Klux Klan, his first question is "Where Am I?". Nobody replies to him. A short while later, the license plate of a car provides the answer: Alabama.

Of the principal cast and crew, eight were also involved in the production of episodes of the original television series: writers Richard Matheson and George Clayton Johnson, composer Jerry Goldsmith, and actors Murray Matheson, Kevin McCarthy, Patricia Barry, William Schallert and Bill Mumy. In addition Buck Houghton, who was producer of the original series for its first three seasons, has a cameo sitting in the diner in Segment 3.

According to John Larroquette, who played one of the lead KKK members, he refused to wear a KKK hood because he wanted his face to be visible.

This is the first collaboration between composer Jerry Goldsmith and co-director Joe Dante which would last for another seven films - one of the longest director/composer relationships on record. These collaborations would also include several productions by Steven Spielberg's companies Amblin Entertainment and Dreamworks Pictures.

Before this movie became an anthology of four stories, Warner Bros. initially explored a single story film idea with the cooperation of Rod Serling's wife Carol Serling.

One of these ideas was Miracle Mile (1988) written by Steve De Jarnatt, who went on to make that film in 1988.

For each of the four segments, each director (Steven Spielberg, John Landis, George Miller and Joe Dante), would use their regular production teams, with Spielberg and Landis acting as producers of the film as an independent production financed by Warner Bros. Richard Matheson was hired to adapt and expand the three stories from the original series.

Joseph Williams, who contributed the song "Anesthesia" for the film, is the son of legendary composer John Williams, who is Steven Spielberg's personal friend and collaborator for the last four decades. Also Jerry Williams, who is John's brother, was the percussionist on the score.

This was Murray Matheson's final film before his death on April 25, 1985 at the age of 72.

This was the final feature for actor Eduard Franz, ending a 35 year film career. He passed away that same year.

During the opening scene, the Lithgow and Brooks begin
to mark their favorite Twilight Zones, soon they reach
Time Enough at Last starring Burgess Meredith, funny as
it is, Meredith starred in that show and supplied the
voice of the narrator in the film.

At one point, the following TV shows are referenced:
Sea Hunt (1958), Perry Mason (1957), Bonanza (1959),
The Real McCoys (1957), The Beverly Hillbillies (1962),
Car 54, Where Are You? (1961), National Geographic
Specials (1965), Gilligan's Island (1964) and Hawaii
Five-O (1968).

Before working on this film, co-director Steven
Spielberg had made his directorial debut on on the
pilot of Rod Serling's post-Twilight Zone work, Night
Gallery (1969).

John Landis' segment "Time Out" was originally entitled
"The Bigot", a story he claimed would retain political
and social commentary of the best Twilight Zone
episodes from the original series.

Technically, this is the second collaboration between
director Steven Spielberg and composer Jerry Goldsmith.

Spielberg "allegedly" had a big hand in Poltergeist
(1982) and oversaw the post-production on that film and
this film.

This film would be the only time that Goldsmith would
work with director John Landis, who had worked with the
late Elmer Bernstein during that time period and was
his composer of choice. He would later work with George
Miller on Babe (1995), and his score was ultimately
replaced by Australian composer Nigel Westlake when the
film's tone changed from its original dark overtones to
family fare.

Goldsmith and Joe Dante would work together frequently
over seven films spanning two decades before
Goldsmith's untimely death in 2004. Goldsmith and
Spielberg would not work together again except in a
producing capacity, as John Williams is his personal
composer.

The spotting sessions for Jerry Goldsmith's landmark score began on December 22, 1982 and did not finish until January of 1983, as each segment was completed. Usually each music track has a slate number listed but in this case it was the initials of each director (Spielberg, Landis, Miller and Dante) for the music in their segment.

Academy Award nominated composer James Newton Howard co-produced the songs "Anesthesia" and "Nights Are Forever" and was also the synthesizer programmer on this film.

The vehicles depicted in the Ku Klux Klan scene provide the dating. With the exception of a Chevrolet, most of them are part of the first generation of the Ford F-Series. This "generation" was in production from 1948 to 1952.

John Larroquette (KKK in segment #1) and Selma Diamond (Mrs.Weinstein in segment #2) would star together again one year later in the NBC sitcom, Night Court.

Cameo
Carol Serling: as the woman who asks "Is there something wrong?" when the flight attendants knock on the airplane restroom door, holding a copy of the Twilight Zone magazine in her arms. She was the wife of Twilight Zone (1959) creator Rod Serling.

Andy House: The Second Assistant Director. Second Assistant directors work primarily on action scenes or getting exterior filler shots, and the tragedy on Segment #1 might have had something to do with this "Smithee" credit.

Just prior to filming, Dan Aykroyd, who plays The Passenger in the film's prologue, married Donna Dixon, who is featured in the "Nightmare at 20,000 Feet" segment, which ends with Aykroyd's appearance as an ambulance driver who comforts John Lithgow's character.

The original conception of the film ending was that, after the segments had been completed, each character would intersect with one another. This idea was mainly scrapped, but it briefly appears as an "epilogue", as Dan Aykroyd's character appears at the very end of the "Nightmare at 20,000 Feet" segment and comforts John Lithgow's character from the segment by playing "The Midnight Special" by Creedence Clearwater Revival, which was also used in the prologue of the film.

Anthony's powers have the sound effects of the Tempest (1983) arcade game.

Series creator Rod Serling made up the phrase "Sixth Dimension" to use in season one's opening narration. William Self of CBS-TV asked him what was the fifth dimension (given that dimensions one through three are exemplified by a line, a plane, and a cube, respectively, and the fourth is time). Serling answered, "I don't know. Aren't there five?" He then changed the narration to "There is a fifth dimension..."

Rod Serling invited any viewers to submit a script. He was flooded with over 14,000 scripts, and he actually got around to reading 500 of them. But only two were any good, and he couldn't use them because they didn't fit the format of the show.

Rod Serling wanted Richard Egan to do the narration because of his rich, deep voice. However, due to strict studio contracts of the time, Egan was unable to. Serling said, "It's Richard Egan or no one. It's

Richard Egan, or I'll do the thing myself," which is exactly what happened.

Rod Serling thought he had come up with the term "Twilight Zone" on his own (he liked the sound of it), but after the show aired he found out that it is an actual term used by Air Force pilots when crossing the day / night sides above the world.

Due to budgetary constraints in its second season, the network decided to cut costs by shooting some episodes on videotape rather than film. Because videotape was a relatively primitive medium in the early 1960s, the editing of tape was next to impossible. Thus, each of the 6 episodes was "camera-cut" as in live TV, on a studio sound stage, using a total of four cameras. The requisite multicamera setup of the videotape experiment, pretty much precluded location shooting, severely limiting the potential scope of the story-lines, and so, the short-lived experiment was ultimately abandoned. The limitations of using videotape (e.g., it could not be edited as cleanly as film and its visual quality was poorer) led them to switch back to film for the rest of the series, despite the greater cost. The 6 videotaped episodes were titled: Twilight Zone: The Lateness of the Hour (1960); Twilight Zone: Static (1961); Twilight Zone: The Whole Truth (1961); Twilight Zone: The Night of the Meek (1960); Twilight Zone: Twenty Two (1961); Twilight Zone: Long Distance Call (1961) and then transferred to film for broadcast, which saved the producers about $5,000 per episode.

CBS wanted Orson Welles as the narrator/host, but the producers felt that he asked for too much money.

Other than series creator, host and narrator Rod Serling, Robert McCord was the only actor to appear in all five seasons. In second place are Jack Klugman, John Anderson, Jon Lormer and Vaughn Taylor, who each appeared in four seasons. Klugman and Taylor both appeared in the first, third, fourth and fifth seasons, Anderson appeared in the first, second, fourth and fifth seasons and Lormer appeared in the each of the first four seasons.

The oft-parodied high-pitched guitar melody riff in the theme music was played by Howard A. Roberts.

Although the phrase "Submitted for your approval" from Rod Serling's opening narration has come to be closely identified with the show (and is often used by Serling impressionists), it is actually heard in only three episodes: Twilight Zone: Cavender Is Coming (1962), Twilight Zone: In Praise of Pip (1963), and Twilight Zone: A Kind of a Stopwatch (1963).

Rod Serling started the series after a teleplay of his became the critically acclaimed Westinghouse Desilu Playhouse: The Time Element (1958).

All episodes in Seasons 1, 2, 3 and 5 were 30 minutes in length. Episodes in Season 4 (airing from January to May 1963) were one hour in length due to CBS' switching the show's available time-slot where only an hour could be taken.

Rod Serling was ranked #1 in TV Guide's list of the "25 Greatest Sci-Fi Legends" (1 August 2004 issue).

A comic book version of this series, "hosted" by the artistic image of Rod Serling, ran until 1982 - long after the real Serling had died.

Of the three "Twilight Zone" TV series over the years, this is the only one which does not include Rod Serling's image during the opening credits. Of course, this is the only one of the series to have the opening voice-over performed by Serling.

Ranked #8 in TV Guide's list of the "25 Top Cult Shows Ever!" (30 May 2004 issue).

On 11 August 2009 the US Postal Service issued a pane of twenty 44¢ commemorative postage stamps honoring early USA television programs. A booklet with 20 picture postal cards was also issued. On the stamp honoring "The Twilight Zone" is a picture of its creator, host/narrator Rod Serling.

Other shows honored in the Early TV Memories issue were: The Adventures of Ozzie & Harriet (1952), Alfred Hitchcock Presents (1955), The Dinah Shore Show (1951), Dragnet (1951), The Ed Sullivan Show (1948), The George Burns and Gracie Allen Show (1950), Hopalong Cassidy (1952), The Honeymooners (1955), The Howdy Doody Show (1947), I Love Lucy (1951), Kukla, Fran and Ollie (1947), Lassie (1954), The Lone Ranger (1949), Perry Mason (1957), The Phil Silvers Show (1955), The Red Skelton Hour (1951), "Texaco Star Theater" (titled Texaco Star Theatre (1948), 1954-1956), The Tonight Show (which began as Tonight! (1953)), and You Bet Your Life (1950).

Alien (1979)
117 min - Horror | Sci-Fi - 22 June 1979 (USA)

The commercial vessel Nostromo receives a distress call
from an unexplored planet. After searching for
survivors, the crew heads home only to realize that a
deadly bioform has joined them.

Director: Ridley Scott
Writers: Dan O'Bannon (story), Ronald Shusett (story)
Stars: Sigourney Weaver, Tom Skerritt, John Hurt

Imitated so many times but never duplicated. Most of
the visuals of the film still hold up (except for Ash's
fake head). The cast all have something to contribute.
The tension is strong, the musical score is perfect and
the chest burster scene is still shocking. Props to the
filmmakers for having a heroine that isn't a timid
damsel in distress. Only surpassed by it's sequel
Aliens

The name of "the company" that the crew work for is
"Weylan-Yutani" (the spelling was changed to "Weyland-
Yutani" in Aliens (1986) and later films). The name can
be seen on a computer monitor, as well as on a beer can
Dallas drinks from during the crew meal. The light-blue
"wings" emblem seen in several places, most notably
Ash's uniform, is intended to be W-Y's logo (the logo
was also changed for the later films).

The horseshoe-shaped alien craft became known by the
nickname "The Big Croissant" among the cast and crew.

The engines of the Narcissus coming to life was created
by having water pour out of showers with strong arc
lights around it. This gave the illusion that it was
plasma.

The production designers, in an attempt to cut costs
while still remaining creative, constructed several of
the sets in such a way as to make them usable in more
than one scene. A good example of this can be seen in
the "Space Jockey" room (the room in which to away team
discovers the skeletal remains in the alien ship) and
the "egg chamber." The sets were designed so that the
skeleton and the revolving disc on which it sits could

be removed and the empty space then redressed with the "eggs," creating, combined with a matching matte painting, a vast cavern full of potential alien spawn.

When the Nostromo crew first discover the marooned alien spacecraft and exit their craft to investigate, the murky POV footage through their helmet visors was filmed by Ridley Scott walking a consumer camcorder at low level across the cramped set.

The large Space Jockey sculpture was designed and painted by H.R. Giger himself, who was disappointed he couldn't put any finishing touches on it by the time filming came about for the scene. Also, the Space Jockey prop was burned and destroyed by a burning cigarette left on the model. Los Angeles. The unfortunate event was covered by local TV news stations that evening.

Yaphet Kotto (Parker) actually picked fights with Bolaji Badejo who played the Alien, in order to help his onscreen hatred of the creature.

The embryonic movements of the facehugger, prior to bursting out of its egg, were created by Ridley Scott using both his rubber-gloved hands.

The vapor released from the top of the spacesuit helmets (presumably exhausted air from the breathing apparatus) was actually aerosol sprayed from inside the helmets. In one case, the mechanism broke and started spraying inside the helmet.

A closer look at the alien eggs in the scene right before the facehugger reveals that slime on the eggs is dripping from bottom to top. Ridley Scott did this intentionally by shooting with the egg hanging from the ceiling and the camera upside down.

At the start of production, Ridley Scott had to contend with 9 producers being onset at all times, questioning the length of time he was taking over each shot.

After the first week of shooting, Dan O'Bannon asked if he could attend the viewing of the dailies, and was somewhat staggered when Gordon Carroll refused him. To get past that ban, O'Bannon viewed the dailies by standing beside the projectionist whilst he screened them for everyone else.

During production an attempt was made to make the alien character transparent or at least translucent.

While he was working on the visual effects for this film, Brian Johnson was simultaneously working in the same capacity on Star Wars: Episode V - The Empire Strikes Back (1980).

According to myth, the name for the company, "Weylan-Yutani" (the spelling was changed to "Weyland-Yutani" in Aliens (1986) and later films), was taken from the names of Ridley Scott's former neighbors - he hated them, so he decided to "dedicate" the name of the "evil company" to them. In reality the name was created by conceptual designer Ron Cobb (who created the Nostromo and the crew's uniforms) to imply a corner on the spacecraft market by an English-Japanese corporation. According to himself, he would have liked to use "Leyland-Toyota" but obviously could not so he changed one letter in Leyland and added the Japanese name of his (not Scott's) neighbor.

The space jockey prop was 26 feet tall.

Entertainment Weekly voted this as the third scariest film of all time.

Much of the dialogue was developed through improvisation.

The computer screen displaying Nostromo's orbit around the planet contains a hidden credit to Dr. Brian Wyvill, one of the programmers for the animation. Within the top frame entitled Deorbital Descent, it is possible to isolate the letters "BLOB", Dr. Brian Wyvill's common nickname.

For the scene in which the facehugger attacks, the egg was upside down above the camera, and the operator thrust it down toward the lens like a hand puppet.

The models had to be repainted every evening of the shoot because the slime used on-set removed the acrylic paint from their surfaces.

Among some of the ingredients of the alien costume are Plasticine and Rolls Royce motor parts.

130 alien eggs were made for the egg chamber inside the downed spacecraft.

An early draft of the script had a male Ripley, making this one of at least three films where Sigourney Weaver played a character originally planned to be a man. The second is The TV Set (2006) and the third is Vantage Point (2008).

The writing partnership between Dan O'Bannon and Ronald Shusett came about when Shusett approached O'Bannon about helping him adapt a Philip K. Dick story that he had acquired the rights to. That was "We Can Remember It for You Wholesale" which later became Total Recall (1990). O'Bannon then said that he had an idea that he was stuck on about an alien aboard a spaceship and that he needed some assistance. Shusett agreed to help out and they tackled the alien movie first as they felt it would have been the cheaper of the two to make.

In a preview of the bonus feature menus for the "Alien Legacy" box set posted to USENET, the bio for Dallas had him as being born female and Lambert as being born male, suggesting gender reassignment before the events in the film. Fan reaction prompted this to be changed before production of the DVDs.

H.R. Giger's design for the Chestburster was originally based very strongly on Francis Bacon's Three Studies for Figures at the Base of a Crucifixion, depicting creatures that while quite phallic are also more birdlike, being based on the Greek Furies. Giger's doubts about his first design were confirmed when Ridley Scott fell about laughing at the sight of the prototype Chestburster, describing it as "like a plucked turkey", and Roger Dicken ended up retooling it to resemble the now classic design.

Bolaji Badejo beat Peter Mayhew to the part of the alien.

In The Blue Planet (2001), David Attenborough said the Alien (1979) monster was modeled after the Phronima, a creature spotted by submersibles at great depths. However there is little evidence to support this claim - the original Alien design was based on a previous painting by H.R. Giger, Necronom IV, which bears little resemblance to the Phronima. Giger's agent, Bijan

Aalam, claims "He never inspired himself by any animals, terrestrial or marine".

Jerry Goldsmith was most aggrieved by the changes that Ridley Scott and his editor Terry Rawlings wrought upon his score. Scott felt that Goldsmith's first attempt at the score was far too lush and needed to be a bit more minimalist. Even then, Goldsmith was horrified to discover that his amended score had been dropped in places by Rawlings who inserted segments from Goldsmith's score to Freud (1962) instead. (Rawlings had initially used these as a guide track only, and ended up preferring them to Goldsmith's revised work.) Goldsmith harbored a grudge against the two right up to his death in 2004.

Dan O'Bannon first encountered H.R. Giger's unique style when the two were briefly working on Alejandro Jodorowsky's ill-fated attempt at making "Dune".

The genesis of the film arose out of Dan O'Bannon's dissatisfaction with his first feature, Dark Star (1974) which John Carpenter directed in 1974. Because of that film's severe low budget, the alien was quite patently a beach ball. For his second attempt, O'Bannon wanted to craft an altogether more convincing specimen. The goofiness of Dark Star (1974) also led him in the direction of an intense horror movie.

Walter Hill's re-write included to make two of the characters female (and to add a romantic subplot that was deleted) and to alter much of the dialogue written by Dan O'Bannon and Ronald Shusett. The original dialogue has been described as poetic but Hill assessed it as pretentious and obscure.

Ranked #7 on the American Film Institute's list of the 10 greatest films in the genre "Sci-Fi" in June 2008.

Three versions of the landing craft were built for the production: a 12" version for long shots, a 48" version for the landing sequence and a seven ton rig for showing the ship at rest on the planet's surface.

A lawsuit by A.E. van Vogt, claiming plagiarism of his 1939 story "Discord in Scarlet" (which he had also incorporated in the 1950 novel "Voyage of the Space Beagle"), was settled out of court.

Carlo Rambaldi constructed three alien heads based on H.R. Giger's designs: two mechanical models for use in various close-up work, and an elementary model for medium-to-long shots. Rambaldi was not available to operate his creations on the actual shoot, though he did spend two weeks in the UK as a technical advisor to Ridley Scott and his crew.

Walter Hill and David Giler's most significant contribution to the script was to make Ash a robot. Although Dan O'Bannon has been reluctant to acknowledge any positive changes by Hill and Giler, Ronald Shusett has described the addition as a significant improvement to the plot.

Alison Bechdel is a cartoonist who, in her comic Dykes to Watch Out For, proposed a simple test to see if a film treated its female characters as equal members of the cast. The rule has three parts: the must feature 1. At least two female characters, who 2. have a conversation with each other that 3. isn't about one of the male characters. This criteria came to be known as the Bechdel test. The character in the comic who outlines these criteria says the last movie she saw that fit these criteria was Alien.

Dallas' pursuit of the alien down the ventilator shafts, and the intercut scenes of the rest of the crew urging him on, was shot in one day.

"Nostromo" is the title of a Joseph Conrad book. The shuttlecraft is called the "Narcissus", from the title of another Joseph Conrad book. See also Aliens (1986).

Like the alien, parasitic wasps gestate inside a host's body; in this case a caterpillar; and then chews its way out with razor sharp teeth. Unlike the human host, however, the caterpillar usually does not die right away. Instead, it has been affected with a virus that changes its behavior. The caterpillar will usually create a cocoon for itself to turn into a butterfly. Under the influence of this virus, however, it spins its cocoon instead around the newly hatched wasp larva, and then aggressively guards the cocoon against other predators. It does this at the expense of seeking out food, so it will eventually starve to death.

Originally to be directed by Walter Hill, but he pulled out and gave the job to Ridley Scott.

Ridley Scott's first exposure to early Alien (1979) drafts were sent to him by Sanford Lieberson, then head of 20th Century Fox's London headquarters. Lieberson had seen Scott's The Duellists (1977) and was adequately impressed to consider the neophyte filmmaker.

Director Ridley Scott and composer Jerry Goldsmith were at odds with each other on the usage of the original music score. As a result, many crucial cues were either rescored, ill-placed, or deleted altogether, and the intended end title replaced with Howard Hanson's "Symphony No. 2 (Romantic)". The original intended score was featured as an isolated track on the now out-of-print 20th Anniversary DVD.

The decal on the door of the Nostromo is a "checkerboard square", the symbol on Purina's pet food label; it designated Alien Chow.

A green monitor visible behind Ripley while the crew discusses Kane's condition outside the kitchen shows nonsense characters as well as the word "Giler", obviously a nod to producer David Giler.

The literal translations of some of this film's foreign language titles include Alien: The Eighth Passenger (Argentina, Mexico, Spain, Canada, Denmark and France) and Alien: The Uncanny Creature from a Strange World (West Germany).

Ridley Scott was keen to take on the project as the one that he had been previously working on at Paramount, Tristan + Isolde (2006), was stuck in development hell.

The producers of the 1950s potboiler It! The Terror from Beyond Space (1958) considered suing for plagiarism but didn't.

When the movie was broadcast in Israel, its title was changed to "The Eighth Passenger" in Hebrew.

Nostromo's identification number is 180924609.

The alien's method of reproduction via implantation was deliberately intended to invoke images of male rape and impregnation. During early development, Dan O'Bannon and Ronald Shusett ran into a writing impasse trying to work out how the alien would get aboard the ship. Shussett came up with the idea, "the alien f*cks one of them!", which was eventually developed into the facehugger concept.

According to screenwriter Dan O'Bannon, the inspiration for the iconic 'chest-burster' scene came from his own experiences with the pain of Crohn's disease.

In the chest bursting scene, Veronica Cartwright, who played Lambert, screamed when blood splattered on her. This wasn't planned, because the cast didn't know which way the blood would splatter.

Ridley Scott originally intended for the alien to be dying when found in the shuttle at the end and ultimately transforming itself into a new egg.

Kay Lenz auditioned for the role of Ripley.

The Facehugger was planned to be painted green, but O'Bannon, seeing the unpainted Facehugger on set and noting how inventive its human flesh-tone color was, argued for it to remain as is.

The room where Stanton's Brett gets taken out by the Xenomorph was a point of contention between Scott and the producers. They didn't understand why there would be water pouring or chains dangling in a ship such as this. Scott, feeling he needed the extra movement in the scene, stuck to his guns and got his chains.

There was discussion to include a gay relationship between Ripley and Lambert.

Before filming the scene where Ash shoves a rolled up magazine into Ripley's mouth, Scott told Weaver actor Ian Holm was going to stick the magazine "up her hooter." Of course, he is referring to her mouth, though Weaver was more than a little confused at the time.

A different version of Ash explaining to the remaining crew what his mission was had much different dialogue. According to Cartwright, Ash originally asked them if they had tried to communicate with the Xenomorph yet. There was also dialogue about the alien being an experiment of some kind.

It was Weaver's idea to sing, "You Are My Lucky Star" while preparing to get rid of the Xenomorph. Scott mentions how much flack he got from the production because of how expensive the rights to the song were.

The character of Ash, and subsequently an android character being introduced into the film, is what O'Bannon calls a "Russian spy," someone on a mission who it is discovered intends to sabotage said mission. "If it wasn't in there, what difference does it make?" the screenwriter asks. "I mean, who gives a rat's ass? So somebody is a robot." O'Bannon was annoyed by the character being added and calls it "an inferior idea from inferior minds well acted and well directed."

Several planned but un-filmed scenes were; Dallas and Parker using a craft called, 'The Flying Bedstead' to enact repairs on the exterior of the ship whilst in space.

A sex scene between Ripley and Dallas.

The crew using internal cameras to look for the alien where they find it halfway matured looking something like a cross between the chest-burster and an egg with feet.

Dallas death was to take place in a huge upside down 'Wind tunnel' in the air duct system. Dallas looked up see the alien on the ceiling of this massive cylinder where it leaped from one side to the other in a super-fast descent toward him.

The alien was to pull Ripley out of the shuttle with the grapple wire where she shoots it with a pistol and makes her way back inside before destroying it with the engines.

Ron Cobb's explanation of the what happened to the Space Jockeys. "At some point a cataclysm causes the extermination of the adults in this unique race, leaving no one to tend and nurture the young. But in a dark lower chamber of the breeding temple a large number of eggs lies dormant, waiting to sense something warm. Years later, the Space Jockey's race comes to this planetoid. The Jockeys are on a mission of exploration and archaeology and they are fascinated by this marvelous temple and unknown culture. One of them finds the egg chamber and gets face-hugged. He's rescued, but no one knows what's happened. They take him back to their ship and continue their exploration of the planet's surface. When the chest-burster erupts from the Jockey it goes on a killing rampage until it is shot and killed. The Alien dies, but immediately decomposes and its acid eats through the hull of the Jockey ship, leaving them stranded on the planet. The Jockeys radio out a message that there is a dangerous parasite on the planet, that nothing can be done to save them in time, and that no one should attempt a rescue. Then the Jockeys slowly starve to death."

Bill Paterson turned down a part.

The Nostromo's computer is named "Mother". The incubation of the alien has also been interpreted as a metaphor for pregnancy.

Ridley Scott reportedly said that originally he wanted a much darker ending. He planned on having the alien bite off Ripley's head in the escape shuttle, sit in her chair, and then start speaking with her voice in a message to Earth.
Apparently, 20th Century Fox wasn't too pleased with such a dark ending.

Extra scenes filmed but not included, due to pacing problems:
The crew listens to the eerie signal from the planetoid.

An additional discussion between Parker and Ripley over the comm, concerning the progress on the Nostromo's engines.

A scene where a furious Lambert hits Ripley for her earlier refusal to let her team back aboard the Nostromo.

An additional conversation between Lambert and Ash, where Lambert notices a dark patch over Kane's lungs on the scanner, foreshadowing Kane's fate.

A discussion among the crew, immediately following Kane's death, on how to proceed further.

Alternative death scene for Brett: Ripley and Parker witness an alive Brett being lifted from the ground.

Ripley and Lambert discuss whether Ash has sex or not.

An unfinished scene where Parker spots the alien next to an airlock door. He asks Ripley and Lambert over the comm to open the airlock and flush the alien into space. However, the alien is warned by a siren and escapes, but not before it gets injured by a door and its blood creates a small hole, causing a short decompression.

Ripley finds Dallas and Brett cocooned. Brett is dead and covered in maggots; Dallas is alive and begs Ripley to kill him. She does so with a flame thrower. The mercy-killing scene would eventually be recycled and used in Alien: Resurrection (1997) when an alien/human-hybrid clone of Ripley begs the real Ripley to kill her, to which she does so with a flame-thrower.

Ash's blood is colored water. Milk was not used as it would have gotten very smelly very quickly under the hot studio lights. Milk was used though for the close-up of his innards, along with pasta and glass marbles.

For the alien's appearance in the shuttle, the set was built around Bolaji Badejo, giving him an effective hiding place. However, extricating himself from the hiding place proved more difficult than anticipated. The alien suit tore several times, and, in one instance, the whole tail came off.

For Parker's death, a fiberglass cast of Yaphet Kotto's head was made, and then filled with pigs' brains. The forehead was made of wax so that the alien's teeth could penetrate it easily. Indeed barbed hooks were fastened to the end of the teeth to make sure it broke the wax surface effectively.

Dan O'Bannon and Ronald Shusett wanted all the characters to be male to avoid what was already becoming a cliché in horror films: the female in danger being the only one left alive to face the killer at the climax, later referred to as the "final girl" phenomena. Ironically, that's exactly where the character of Ripley ended up although it must be noted she is much stronger and more resourceful than the typical horror film "final girl".

Body Count: 9 (including the Space Jockey, facehugger, and the Alien itself).

Lamberts off-screen death according to the novel was supposed to be the Alien forcing her body into a vent too small for it.

Before "Alien," screenwriter Dan O'Bannon had written "Dark Star," an essentially comic treatment of the same plot, for director John Carpenter. His idea to rework it as a thriller/horror movie was the genesis of "Alien." He and writing partner Ronald Shusett pitched it to studios as "'Jaws' in space."

The cargo ship, the Nostromo, took its name from a Joseph Conrad novel.

H.R. Giger's initial designs for the xenomorph were so disturbing that his sketches were held up in customs at the Los Angeles airport. O'Bannon had to go the airport and explain to customs officials that they were designs for a horror movie.

Giger made a point of designing the creature without eyes, so that it would look even more chilling and soulless.

Veronica Cartwright had read for the part of Ripley but didn't realize she was to play Lambert instead until she arrived in London for costume fittings.

As a child, Cartwright had co-starred in another classic creature feature, Alfred Hitchcock's "The Birds." One of her co-stars in that movie was comic actor Doodles Weaver, uncle of Cartwright's future "Alien" co-star, Sigourney Weaver.

Weaver was all but unknown as a film actress when she auditioned. She was the last of the seven principal stars to be cast.

In an early draft of the film was a sex scene between Ripley and Dallas (Tom Skerritt), but it was never filmed.

Also never filmed: an ending in which Ripley's final confrontation with the alien ends with the creature biting off her head.

Ash, which proved a breakthrough role for Ian Holm after 20 previous films, was not initially supposed to be an android. The idea of making him a robot came from producers Walter Hill and David Giler.

For long shots involving the astronaut landing party, Scott and cinematographer Derek Vanlint put their own children in space suits to make the humans appear smaller next to the remains of the Space Jockey, the extraterrestrial pilot whose corpse is found in an empty ship on the planet's surface. The body was already 26 feet tall.

The space suits were bulky and poorly ventilated, so much so that the actors tended to pass out from heat exhaustion. A nurse had to be kept on hand to supply them with oxygen. Only after Scott and Vanlint's children found the suits unbearably hot and passed out as well did the filmmakers modify the costumes to make breathing easier.

The alien's various incarnations came by their slimy, pungent appearance honestly. The "facehugger" creature was made from clams, oysters, and other seafood. The alien that bursts forth from Kane included organ parts from a butcher shop and smelled of formaldehyde.

The actors didn't know in advance how the scene of the alien's emergence from John Hurt's abdomen would play; Scott deliberately kept it a secret so that their horrified reactions would be spontaneous and real.

"All it said in the script was, 'The thing emerges,'" Weaver recalled later, adding that the crew's garb should have given the actors a clue. "Everyone was wearing raincoats," she said. "We should have been a little suspicious."

The fake torso containing the "chestburster" creature was bolted to the dining room table. Hurt was underneath the table with his head sticking up. Camera trickery made it look like his head was attached to the torso.

When the alien burst forth, stagehands pumped geysers of fake blood through the cavity. A jet hit Cartwright in the face, and she passed out.

To scare "Jonesy" (who was actually played by four different cats), the filmmakers hid a German Shepherd behind a screen, then suddenly removed the screen.

Scott meant for the full-grown alien to have a lanky and angular form that no human frame would possess. In fact, there was a man inside the suit, a 22-year-old Nigerian design student named Bolaji Badejo who stood 7' 2". Scott cast him after one of the production crew members met him in a bar.

Badejo had to stand on the set all day; his costume wasn't built to allow him to sit. A special sling was constructed to hoist him so that he could rest his feet.

The slime dripping from the alien's jaws was made of K-Y jelly.

The film's cost has been disputed; differing reports place it anywhere from $8.4 million to $14 million. Nonetheless, it was hugely profitable. It grossed some $81 million in the United States. Its foreign grosses have also been disputed, with the film reportedly earning anywhere from $24 million to $123 million overseas.

"Alien" won an Oscar for Best Visual Effects and was nominated for another, for Best Art Direction.

In 2003, a longer version dubbed "Alien: The Director's Cut" was released, but Scott dismissed the title as a mere marketing tool, said the additional scenes were superfluous, and claimed the original version of the film was "pretty flawless."

The Alien script started out as a bare bones, half story written by Dan O'Bannon and was shopped around for years before several re-writes (by several parties). The story eventually became a collaborative effort that added an android, changed crew names, Ripley's sex, and the entire ending. Saying it "helps him think on paper and pin down what he's doing," Ridley Scott storyboarded the full movie, which doubled the budget.

Scott was "the fifth or sixth director." He didn't know why he was chosen--"not a science fiction guy." Scott said he was a fan of story writer, Dan O'Bannon's (with John Carpenter) Dark Star and knew Dan would have loved to direct. The director wanted it to be "the most straight forward, unpretentious riveting thriller like Psycho or Rosemary's Baby, or even the most brilliant B level like Night of the Living Dead and Texas Chainsaw Masacre, but I want it to look--and I'm going to do this--like 2001. We're going to watch together, all the classic scare movies so I can get the rhythm of how scares work." Scott decided to keep it minimal, "...like the shark, don't show too much of the monster."

Executive Producer and writer Ronald Shusett related that the title sequence was originally bits of flesh and bone coming together to form the word, "Alien," but it was decided to be too gory. Ridley Scott came up with the idea of the word being hieroglyphic; "something...but you don't know what it is."

O'Bannon said the corridors were built without blind corners--he insisted they be put in. They wanted the feeling of an old, battered ship; Scott wanted the set to be circular ("beautiful, but more expensive"). With a small budget, the corridors were scavenged from parts found in aircraft graveyards, assembled like sculpture and painted. When the ship landed on the planetoid, O'Bannon said it came very close to how he wrote it. He thought it would be novel to show the horrendous, dangerous process of landing, with the ship groaning and shaking, wrenching, and was very gratified by how it came out on film.

Scott highly recommended producers David Giler and Gordon Carroll; with them, "You'll find every party in town." The director acknowledged he is very meticulous about casting, saying "If you cast right, about fifty percent of your problems are over." Everyone was nervous, they were very close to production and the lead had not been cast. One night, they (producers and Scott) decided to have dinner at a Japanese restaurant, suggested by Sigourney Weaver. The actress had been doing a lot of theater Off-Broadway. Scott described meeting Weaver: "This beautiful giant walked into the

room...in she walked (before even speaking) and that
was it." Weaver was surprised at the revelation and
added, "I was wearing my hooker boots, so that helped."
They did a whole test run through of the movie with
Sigourney and ran it for 20th Century Fox President,
Alan "Laddie" Ladd Jr. Ladd told them to pick a bunch
of girls from the office (secretaries, assistants,
etc.) and run it for them--see what they think. The
ladies all gave good comments--with one of them saying
that Weaver was like Jane Fonda--and so Ladd gave the
film the go-ahead with the actress starring as Ripley.

On the very first day of shooting, Scott noticed Jon
Finch (Kane 1.0) didn't look well (but didn't say
anything because he thought "Finch was just naturally
pale"). Finally, Scott asked how he was and Finch said
"Not well"; medics were called over and the actor had
to be carried out and taken to the hospital. It turned
out Finch had an extreme case of diabetes--he was out
of the film. At lunch time, Scott reconvened with his
team and they tried to figure out who they could get.
As it turned out their first choice for Kane, John
Hurt, was in London. Hurt relayed that he had
previously been asked to do the film but was
unavailable, scheduled to do a film in South Africa.
Strangely, he wasn't allowed to enter the country. Hurt
said he believed he was confused with actor, John
Heard, who was (put on a list as) undesired because he
disagreed with apartheid (Hurt: "Well, none of us
do."). Hurt came back home. When they met, Scott
pitched the film to Hurt until 12 at night...the actor
was on set at 7 a.m. the next morning.

Editor, Terry Rawlings said that although he thought
Jerry Goldsmith (Chinatown, The Omen, Planet of the
Apes [1968], Total Recall, The Boys from Brazil) a
genius, they didn't always agree with the composer's
score. Instead of what Goldsmith submitted for Alien's
ending, they used his music from Freud; this angered
Goldsmith. The score was nominated for a Golden Globe,
BAFTA and a Grammy Award.

Ridley Scott described a guy crouched down, "wobbling"
the actors' seats (to simulate engine thrust), saying
it irritated people and that everyone rolled their
eyes. "Every step you make, everyone's a Doubting
Thomas." Scott said he "...wondered how many people
fall by the wayside because you can't push your point
home and don't quite get what you want. Nobody respects
you later for having been a nice guy and given up--you
have to get what you want now, because you're going to
wear what you got. You can be very unpopular on the
root, but if you're right, all is forgiven."

The director described the planetoid set as "not so
good." There was a little clump of rocks, only about a
foot high and they just kept circling around them until
he thought it was time to go in. He had someone get a
domestic tape camera, used that, then fed the footage
back into a film camera to get the effect and scale of
the sculpture to look like more than it was. Scott said
artist H. R. Giger's (Swiss surrealist influenced by
Dalí) illustrations were fantastic, but when translated
onto film, they sometimes looked "too fancy." The
director liked it better when they got inside (the
ship), saying the helmet lights helped a lot, so it
didn't look like a set.

Dry ice was one of the most useful effects, but it
sucks oxygen out of tubes--they'd get out of breath
even though they were assured it was safe. Of Scott,
O'Bannon said, "Ridley is a master of atmosphere,
texturing the scene. Without it, the movie would have
been a much lesser picture." The director went to a
great deal of trouble with lighting to make set look
like Giger's drawings/paintings. He made sure the smoke
was uniformly distributed. "People walked around with
incense burners filling the area with smoke, then Scott
himself waved cardboard around to distribute the smoke

so it looked like thickened air, not just billowing
smoke. Finally, he lit it perfectly--elaborate and
careful lighting, with blue gray tone."

With no technology or the money to run air into the
space suits or helmets, there were lots of problems--
condensation, heat, the actors would become short of
air or claustrophobic. Tom Skerritt (Dallas) and
Veronica Cartwright (Lambert) said they damned near
suffocated; that they were supposed to have oxygen
(pumped in by tanks), but that the tanks would
malfunction. Cartwright described the actors walking
around in the suits and helmets, having to carry oxygen
tanks, wearing heavy, painted hockey gloves and boots.
She said they were practically passing out all the
time.

Scott described basing the alien in nature; whatever
the alien would drop onto, it would take on those
characteristics (dropped onto a human, it would look
like a human, dropped onto an ostrich, it looks like an
ostrich). He described watching footage of "a slice of
bark--which, in our terms, to a human being, would be
about 12 feet thick--and there's a grub underneath the
bark, between the bark and the tree. There's always a
space between the bark and the tree. Across the top of
the bark was this insect, which passes over the grub,
stops, backs up, and "feels" the grub is there let's
say, the equivalent of 8 foot below you. It goes up on
its hind legs, produces a needle from between its legs,
and drills through the bark and bulls-eyes right into
the grub and lays its seed, so that the grub becomes
the host of the insect. And does what comes out of the
union between the grub and the insect, does that become
a version of both? That's what we basically went along
with."

Anton Furst (Batman [1989], Full Metal Jacket, Awakenings) ran the laser beams in the egg chamber, an effect Scott was "blown away with." (Furst, who won an Academy Award for his Batmobile design, committed suicide in 1991.) The inside of the egg was made of steamed cattle and sheep parts (delivered fresh every morning) and the fluttering movement caused by Ridley Scott's surgical-gloved hand moving around.

Once they'd gotten going, with some money to start filming, O'Bannon (in LA) contacted Giger (in Switzerland--O'Bannon met Giger while working on a failed production of Dune). O'Bannon wrote out simple parameters of what the facehugger was--a small octopus-like thing that would leap onto someone's face, wrap tentacles around a person's head-- and it would have an organ depositor, which it would shove down a person's throat. A few weeks later, Giger mailed photographic transparencies that came through customs (who didn't understand what they were and were alarmed so O'Bannon had to personally go to LAX to pick them up). He finally got the photographs, held them up to light and was stunned at what he saw. Instead of tentacles, there were fingers. As soon as O'Bannon saw those, "he knew he'd do whatever he had to to get it on film." After conferring with Scott on what the director wanted (Scott pointed to one of Giger's drawings) O'Bannan set himself up at a drawing board and drew a human head, then all views of the facehugger, copying Giger carefully. Concept Artist Ron Cobb helped O'Bannon draw out how the fingers would connect to the body, then O'Bannon finished it. After getting Scott's approval, the drawing was delivered to sculptors. A few days later they had a clay sculpture, made a cast of it and noted it was the color of human skin. Thinking it novel and unusual, instead of painting the cast they left it flesh-colored.

As to the alien itself, as soon as O'Bannon showed Scott Giger's Necronomicon, the director knew it was what he wanted. Bolaji Badejo (a student) was discovered in a bar--he was just the right size (7' 2") to pull off the look.

The dinner scene was played as if nothing was going to happen. Tom Skerritt had seen how it was set up, so he had an idea, but the rest of the cast was kept "locked away." Four cameras were set up and the scene was done in one take. Veronica Cartwright was told she was going to get a little blood on her face. Everyone loved the look on Veronica's face; her reaction was completely real. There was a guy on a skateboard under the table who had the alien on a dolly and whipped it out of the room.

Scott used a German Shepherd on a leash to get the hissing reaction from Jones (the cat) right before the alien kills Brett (Harry Dean Stanton).

O'Bannon didn't want the typical film where the alien was bullet-proof, with ammunition bouncing around in the ship--but they needed a reason why the alien couldn't simply be killed. Concept Artist, Ron Cobb came up with the idea of it bleeding acid that would burn through metal--then they couldn't kill the alien because it would melt through everything, the ship would lose oxygen and they would all die.

Though analysis over the intention of particular sexual connotations continues on, Scott himself described Ash's method of trying to kill Ripley as suppressed/inexpressible desire. The director liked the idea that Ash always sort of wanted to, but didn't have the part to have sex, so he does it with a magazine.

Ash's innards were were pasta, thin rubber tubes, glass marbles, cheap caviar and milk.

Scott said Veronica (Lambert) was great at being two steps away from complete terror and a heart attack. In fact, the director had planned for Lambert to crawl away, hiding in a locker and to die of a heart attack. The shot of the alien's tail going between Lambert's legs is actually footage of Harry Dean Stanton's legs.

The film was meant to be over when Ripley goes into the ship, with the explosions (graphic design on a card!) and the ending score, but Scott said he couldn't possibly end it there. He asked the studio for four more days to add a fourth act, saying "It will change the way film is made" (referring to audiences thinking it's the end, but wait, there's another end!). Weaver asked not to be told what was going to happen so she would be surprised. The actress said they wanted to have more of a quasi-sex scene, but someone from Fox came and gave them a a stern look, telling them they had two days left to finish. Weaver wanted the alien to come and look at Ripley and be kind of turned on by her softness, but Scott said he never thought about the alien in that way. It was Sigourney's idea to sing something (You Are My Lucky Star) to herself, to hang onto her own sanity.

The rumor that the cast, except for John Hurt, did not know what would happen during the chestburster scene is partly true. The scene had been explained for them, but they did not know specifics. For instance, Veronica Cartwright did not expect to be sprayed with blood.

Shredded condoms were used to create tendons of the beast's ferocious jaws

According to Yaphet Kotto, Ridley Scott told him to annoy Sigourney Weaver off-camera so that there would be tension between their characters. Kotto regrets this because he really liked Weaver.

Harrison Ford turned down the role of Captain Dallas.

The inside of the alien eggs as seen by Kane was composed of real organic material. Director Ridley Scott used cattle hearts and stomachs. The tail of the facehugger was sheep intestine.

The chestbursting scene was filmed in one take with four cameras.

The dead facehugger that Ash autopsies was made using fresh shellfish, four oysters and a sheep kidney to recreate the internal organs.

Ridley Scott cites three films as the shaping influences on his movie: Star Wars: Episode IV - A New Hope (1977) and 2001: A Space Odyssey (1968) for their depiction of outer space, and Tobe Hooper's The Texas Chain Saw Massacre (1974) (1974) for its treatment of horror.

Ridley Scott stated that in casting the role of Ripley, it ultimately came down to Sigourney Weaver and Meryl Streep. The two actresses had been schoolmates at Yale.

The creature is never filmed directly facing the camera due to the humanoid features of its face. Ridley Scott, determined at all costs to dispel any notion of a man in a rubber suit, filmed the beast in varying close-up angles of its ghastly profile, very rarely capturing the beast in its entirety.

Copywriter Barbara Gips came up with the famed tagline: "In space, no one can hear you scream."

In H.R. Giger's original illustrations the creature has eyes. For the movie, Giger insisted that the creature have no eyes, thus giving the bleak appearance of a cold and emotionless beast.

20th Century Fox doubled the budget from $4.2 million to $8.4 million on the strength of seeing Ridley Scott's storyboards.

The front (face) part of the alien costume's head is made from a cast of a real human skull.

A scene originally cut, but re-inserted for the Director's Cut shows Lambert slapping Ripley in retaliation for Ripley's refusal to let her, Dallas, and Kane back on the ship. According to both Ridley Scott and Veronica Cartwright, every time she went to slap Sigourney Weaver, Sigourney would shy away. After about three or four takes of this, Scott finally told Cartwright "Not to hold back. Really hit her." Thus the very real shocked reactions of Weaver, Yaphet Kotto, and Harry Dean Stanton.

Many of the interior features of the Nostromo came from airplane graveyards.

The first day that she shot a scene involving Jones the cat, Sigourney Weaver's skin started reacting badly. Horrified, the young actress immediately thought that she might be allergic to cats, and that it would be easier for the production to recast her instead of trying to find 4 more identical cats. As it transpired, Weaver was reacting to glycerin sprayed on her skin to make her look hot and sweaty.

The original cut of the film ran 3 hours and 12 minutes.

Dan O'Bannon's original draft title was "Star Beast", but he was never happy with this. It was only after re-reading his script that he noted how many times the word "alien" appeared, and realized that it was a perfect title: it works as both a noun and an adjective, and it had never been used before.

Ridley Scott did all the hand-held camera-work himself.

For the awakening from hypersleep segment, Veronica Cartwright and Sigourney Weaver had to wear white surgical tape over their nipples so as not to offend certain countries.

Conceptual artist H.R. Giger's designs were changed several times because of their blatant sexuality.

In an interview for Métal Hurlant, Ridley Scott revealed that to make the action more realistic, the flight deck was wired so that flipping a switch in at one console would trigger lights somewhere else. The cast then developed "work routines" for themselves where one would trip a switch, leading another to respond to the changes at his work station and so on.

When casting the role of Ripley, Ridley Scott invited several women from the production office to watch screen tests, and thus gain a female perspective. The women were unanimously impressed with then-unknown actress Sigourney Weaver, whose screen presence they compared to Jane Fonda's.

After the crew awakens from hyper-sleep, the navigator Lambert announces that the ship is "just short of Zeta 2 Reticuli". Zeta Reticuli is a real double-star system about 39 light-years from Earth, and has figured prominently in UFO lore. In the 1960s, Barney and Betty Hill claimed to have been abducted by "gray" aliens from Zeta Reticuli.

The chestbursting scene was considered the second scariest movie moment of all time on Bravo's The 100 Scariest Movie Moments (2004).

All of the names of the main characters were changed multiple times by Walter Hill and David Giler during revisions of the original script by Dan O'Bannon and Ronald Shusett. The script by O'Bannon and Shusett also had a clause indicating that all of the characters are "unisex", meaning they could be cast with male or female actors; consequently, all of the characters are only referred to by their last name (Dallas, Kane, Ripley, Ash, Lambert, Parker, and Brett), and the few gender-specific pronouns (he/she) were corrected after casting. However, Shusett and O'Bannon never thought of casting Ripley as a female character.

The movie's Hungarian title translated back mean "The 8th passenger is the Death", and all other Alien movies likewise had titles that end with the word "death". Aliens (1986): "The name of the planet: Death"; Alien³ (1992): "Final solution: Death"; Alien: Resurrection (1997): "The Resurrestion of Death". The original releases ignored the word "Alien" from the title, but it has since been retroactively inserted back after more people became familiar with the franchise's English name. Despite this, the Alien is again referred to as "Death" in the Hungarian title of AVP: Alien vs. Predator (2004): "The Death against The Predator".

Ridley Scott's original cut was a lot bloodier, but because of the negative reactions of test audience and possibility that movie will get X rating, scenes with violence and gore were cut down. Some outtakes that can be seen in making of documentaries show longer and bloodier versions of chestburster scene and Brett's death scene.

According to John Hurt in the DVD Documentary, he was considered at the beginning of casting to play Kane but had already committed to another film that was set to take place in South Africa, so Jon Finch got the role instead. However, two separate incidents occurred which got Hurt the role. First was the fact that he was banned from South Africa because the country mistook him for actor John Heard who strongly opposed the Apartied (Hurt points out that he was opposed to it too, but was lucky enough not to get blacklisted) so he was unable to do the other film. Second, Finch became seriously ill from diabetes and had to pull out. Ridley Scott immediately contacted Hurt, pitched him the script over a weekend and Hurt arrived on the set Monday morning with little to no sleep to begin filming.

Conceptual artist H.R. Giger would successfully sue 20th Century Fox 18 years later over his lack of screen credit on Alien: Resurrection (1997).

Potential directors, who either were considered by the studio or wanted to direct, included Robert Aldrich, Peter Yates, Jack Clayton, Dan O'Bannon and Walter Hill. Aldrich in particular came very close to being hired, but the producers ultimately decided against it after they met him in person, and it quickly became apparent that he had no real enthusiasm for the project beyond the money he would have received. According to David Giler, the moment when Aldrich talked himself out of the job came when they asked him what kind of a design he had in mind for the facehugger; Aldrich simply shrugged and said "We'll put some entrails on the guy's face. It's not as if anyone's going to remember that critter once they've left the theater."

Originally, no film companies wanted to make this film, 20th Century-Fox had even passed on it. They stated various reasons, most being that it was too bloody. The only producer who wanted to make the film was Roger Corman, and it was not until Walter Hill came on board that it all changed. 20th Century-Fox agreed to make the film as long as the violence was toned down; even after that they still rejected the first cut for being "too bloody".

Aside from being an easy-to-remember moniker for the ship's computer, another reason for the crew referring to it as "Mother" is the actual name of the computer: MU-TH-UR. This is printed in red lettering on the small access door that holds the computer card that Dallas and Ripley use to gain
access to the control console room.

The screen test that bagged Sigourney Weaver the role of Ripley was her speech from her final scene.

The Nostromo is supposed to be 800 feet long, while the craft she is towing is a mile and a half long.

Roger Dicken, who designed and operated the facehugger and the chestburster, had originally wanted the latter to pull itself out of Kane's torso with its own little hands, a sequence he felt would have produced a much more horrifying effect than the gratuitous blood and guts in the release print.

According to Ridley Scott in the DVD commentary, he had envisioned a moment in the ending scenes of Ripley and the alien in the space shuttle in which the alien would be sexually aroused by Ripley. Scott says that in the scene, after Ripley hides in the closet, the alien would find her and would be staring at her through the glass door. The alien would then start touching itself as if comparing its body to Ripley's. The idea was eventually scrapped.

20th Century Fox Studios almost did not allow the "space jockey", or the giant alien pilot, to be in the film. This was because, at the time, props for movies weren't so large and it would only be used for one scene. However, conceptual artist 'Ron Cobb (I)' convinced them to leave the scene in the movie, as it would be the film's "Cecil. B. DeMille shot", showing the audience that this wasn't some low-budget B-movie.

There is no dialog for the first 6 minutes.

During the opening sequence, as the camera wanders around the corridors of the Nostromo, we can clearly see a Krups coffee grinder mounted to a wall; this is the same model that became the "Mr. Fusion" in Back to the Future (1985).

Ridley Scott's 2003 director's cut largely came about when over 100 boxes of footage of his 1979 original were discovered in a London vault.

Three aliens were made: a model; a suit for seven-footer Bolaji Badejo; and another suit for a trained stunt man.

According to Ridley Scott, the mechanism that was used to make the alien egg open was so strong, that it could tear off a hand.

The grid-like flooring on the Nostromo was achieved using upturned milk crates, painted over.

The character of Ash did not appear in Dan O'Bannon's original script.

The stylized artwork that Ridley Scott used to create the storyboards that got Fox to double the budget were inspired by the artwork of famed French comic book artist Jean Giraud AKA Moebius.

The screech of the newborn alien was voiced by animal impersonator Percy Edwards. He was personally requested by director Ridley Scott to do the sound effect and it was recorded in one take.

To simulate the thrust of engines on the Nostromo, Ridley Scott had crew members shake and wobble the seats the actors were sitting in.

Dan O'Bannon was hyper-critical of any changes made to his script and, to be fair, he defended some aspects of the film that ended up being most iconic (including H.R. Giger's designs). Although he would come on set and nitpick, O'Bannon was generally welcomed by Ridley Scott until O'Bannon lost his temper and insulted Scott in front of the whole crew. The producers, including Walter Hill, had minimal respect for O'Bannon and largely ignored him, giving him little credit once the film became a success.

The alien's habit of laying eggs in the chest (which later burst out) was inspired by spider wasps, which are said to lay their eggs "in the abdomen of spiders." This image gave Dan O'Bannon nightmares, which he used to create the story. But spider wasps (pompilidae) lay eggs on their prey, not inside them, after which the wasp maggots simply snack on the sting-paralyzed spiders. O'Bannon may instead have been thinking of either ichneumon wasps or braconid wasps. The ichneumon drills a single egg into a wood-boring beetle larva, whereas braconids inject eggs inside certain caterpillars. Both result in fatal hatch-outs more alike to O'Bannon's alien.

The original name for the spaceship was Snark. This was later changed to Leviathan before they finally settled for Nostromo.

During this production, only H.R. Giger and Bolaji
Badejo were permitted to view the rushes with Ridley
Scott, enabling them to better discuss and refine
aspects of the beast's look and movements.

To preserve the shock-value of the alien's appearance,
no production images of it were released, not even to
author Alan Dean Foster when he wrote the film's
novelization.

Dan O'Bannon requested that Ridley Scott and producer
Walter Hill, both of whom had little knowledge of
horror or science-fiction cinema, screen The Texas
Chain Saw Massacre (1974) to prepare for shooting the
more intense scenes. Scott and Hill were stunned by the
horror film and admitted it motivated them to ratchet
up the intensity of their own film.

When Ripley punches in the code to activate the scuttle
procedure, one of the button tabs reads AGARIC FLY.
While engineering sounding in name, fly agaric is
actually a highly poisonous hallucinogenic mushroom
whose toxin used to be commonly used in flypaper.

Aliens (1986)
137 min - Action | Adventure | Sci-Fi - 18 July
1986 (USA)
The planet from Alien (1979) has been colonized, but
contact is lost. This time, the rescue team has
impressive firepower, but will it be enough?

Director: James Cameron
Writers: James Cameron (story), David Giler (story)
Stars: Sigourney Weaver, Michael Biehn, Carrie Henn

-A Couple Of Average Joe's
The first great sequel that makes female characters
just as badass as their male counterparts. Aliens takes
what worked in the original and blow everything out of
the water. Sigourney Weaver totally earns her first
Oscar nomination and the support cast backs her every
play. Beautiful set designs and creature effects. The
awesome battle with the alien queen is only surpassed
by James Horner's powerful score.

The knife trick scene was not in the original shooting
script. According to Lance Henriksen, the adding of
Hudson's hand to the knife trick was discussed with
almost everyone, except Bill Paxton.

When filming the scene with Newt in the duct, Carrie
Henn kept deliberately blowing her scene so she could
slide down the vent, which she later called a slide
three stories tall. James Cameron finally dissuaded her
by saying that if she completed the shot, she could
play on it as much as she
wanted. She did, and he kept his promise.

Like most films, the movie wasn't shot in sequence. But
for added realism, James Cameron filmed the scene where
we first meet the Colonial Marines (one of the earliest
scenes) last. This was so that the camaraderie of the
Marines was realistic because the actors had spent
months filming together.

Whilst filming the power loader battle. The crew played
a practical joke on Sigourney Weaver by strategically
strapping a balloon connected to an air pipe to where
her backside would be. When they pumped up the balloon,

Sigourney thought that the man operating the power loader inside it was getting aroused behind her.

The Alien nest set was kept intact after filming. It was later used as the Axis Chemicals set for Batman (1989). When the Batman crew first entered the set, they found most of the Alien nest still intact.

When they have landed and deployed in the troop carrier, Apone tells the Marines they have 10 seconds until they arrive. If you count from here until the first Marine jumps out of the carrier and his boots hit the ground, it really is ten seconds.

In both the standard and special edition versions, the fifteen minute countdown at the end of the film is indeed fifteen minutes.

Sigourney Weaver's Best Actress Academy Award nomination for this movie was the first ever for an actress in an action role in an action movie.

According to Bill Paxton, he improvised much of his lines including "Game over, man! Game over!"

Lance Henriksen had privately pledged to quit acting if this part didn't work out for him after years of journeyman roles. It proved to be one of his most successful films.

The spear gun Ripley used at the end of Alien is
briefly visible in the opening scenes of Aliens - still
stuck at the bottom of the escape pod door where it
jammed 57 years earlier.

Al Matthews, who plays a Marine sergeant in this film,
was in real life the first black Marine to be promoted
to the rank of sergeant in the field during service in
Vietnam.

Sigourney Weaver had initially been very hesitant to
reprise her role as Ripley, and had rejected numerous
offers from Fox Studios to do any sequels, fearing that
her character would be poorly written, and a sub-par
sequel could hurt the legacy of Alien (1979). However,
she was so impressed by the high quality of James
Cameron's script - specifically, the strong focus on
Ripley, the mother-daughter bond between her character
and Newt, and the incredible precision with which
Cameron wrote her character, that she finally agreed to
do the film.

Budget constraints meant that they could only afford to
have six hypersleep capsules for the scenes set aboard
the Sulaco. Clever placement of mirrors and camera
angles made it look like there were 12. Each hypersleep
chamber cost over $4,300 to build.

The alien screams are Baboon shrieks altered in post.

Sigourney Weaver had several notes for James Cameron
after having read the script. However, Cameron praised
her for never taking issue with the direction he wanted
to take with the story. Her notes were all about how
she felt Ripley should respond to her situations, which
he was happy to accommodate.

Having hired James Cameron to write the screenplay,
20th Century Fox then did the unthinkable when he left
the production to direct The Terminator (1984): they
agreed to wait for Cameron to become available again
and finish the screenplay. Cameron had only completed
about 90 pages at that stage, but the studio had loved
what he had written so far.

One of the alien eggs used in the film is now exhibited in the Smithsonian Institute in Washington, D.C.

The "special edition" includes extra scenes: Newt's parents discovering the abandoned alien ship on LV-426, scenes of Ripley discussing her daughter, Hudson bragging about his weaponry, robot sentry guns repelling first alien raid, and Hicks and Ripley exchanging first names. Also included is a scene on LV-426 where a child rides a low-slung tricycle similar to one ridden in The Terminator (1984), also directed by James Cameron.

When Newt and Ripley are locked in MedLab, Ripley is attacked by one of the two facehuggers after setting off the sprinklers, resulting in the facehugger wrapping its tail around her neck after jumping off of a table leg. To film this, director James Cameron had the Special Effects crew design a facehugger fully capable of walking towards Ripley on its own, but to make it appear as if it jumps off of the table, and Cameron then used backwards-filming. He set up the facehugger on the table leg, then dragged it off and later edited the piece of film to play backward to make it appear to be moving forward towards Ripley. The crew thought that the fact that water was falling down during this whole scene would affect the sequence that was filmed backward (it would show the water moving up instead of down). In the end, the water was not visible enough to see the direction in which it was falling.

The difficulties surrounding Sigourney Weaver's contract negotiations were such that James Cameron and Gale Anne Hurd - recently married - announced that if the deal was not done by the time they got back from their honeymoon, they were out. When they returned, no progress had been made - so James Cameron, determined to make the film and wary of the deadline scenario he had created, devised a scheme: he telephoned Arnold Schwarzenegger's agent for an informal chat and informed him that, thanks to his newfound standing in Hollywood following The Terminator (1984), he had decided to make this film entirely his own by writing Ripley out; as Cameron anticipated, Schwarzenegger's agent immediately relayed the information to his colleague representing Weaver at ICM, who in turn contacted 20th Century-Fox Head of Production Lawrence Gordon; both men, determined that under no circumstances whatsoever would Ripley be written out, wasted no time in sealing Weaver's deal.

Bishop's line about him being incapable of hurting a person or letting anyone come to harm are a paraphrase of Isaac Asimov's Three Laws of Robotics, more specifically the First Law: "A robot may not injure a human being nor, through inaction, allow a human being to come to harm." (the Second Law is "A robot must obey the orders given by a human being except where it would conflict with the First Law; the Third Law is, "A robot must protect its own existence except where it would conflict with the First or Second Laws."). Asimov eventually introduced a "Zeroth" Law: "A robot may not injure humanity nor, through inaction, allow humanity to come to harm."

To bring the alien queen to life would take anything between 14 and 16 operators.

None of the models or the original designs of the Narcissus (the Nostromo's shuttle) from Alien (1979) could be found, so set designers and model-makers had to reconstruct the model of the ship and the interior set from watching Alien (1979).

Most of the movie was filmed under very bluish light to give it a strange and "alien" feel. The colors of the Marines' camouflage BDUs and the Humbrol "Brown Bess" used on the Pulse Rifles were all chosen specifically to work with the blue set lighting. As a result, both look very different under natural light than they did on screen.

In a deleted scene, the portrait of Ripley's daughter is of Elizabeth Inglis, Sigourney Weaver's real-life mother.

There was talk of bringing H.R. Giger back for the second movie to do more design work, but James Cameron decided against it because there was only one major design to be done, the Alien Queen and Cameron had already done some of the drawings for the character.

Aliens (1986) was never shown to test audiences because editing was not completed until the week before its theatrical release.

The word "fuck" is used 25 times in the film, 18 of them are spoken by Hudson.

Except for a very small reference in Alien (1979), the special edition of this film is the first to reveal the name of 'The Company' as Weyland-Yutani. The name is clearly written on several pieces of equipment and walls in the colony during a pre-alien outbreak scene of the special edition.

According to Lance Henriksen, during the production of "Aliens", the film Full Metal Jacket (1987) was also being shot at a nearby location. Because of this the crews of each movie would often gather together for parties.

Lance Henriksen wanted to wear double-pupil contact lenses for a scene where Bishop is working in the lab on a microscope and gives a scary look at one of the Marines. He came to set with those lenses, but James Cameron decided he did not need to wear them because he was acting the character with just the right amount of creepiness already.

The assault vehicle is a modified tow-truck that British Airways used for towing airplanes around at Heathrow. The only trouble was that the truck they purchased weighed 75 tons. By stripping out most of the lead used in its construction, they were able to remove about 30 tons.

When Ripley confronts Burke about having the Jordens sent out to check the grid reference, she tells him she checked the company log reference 6.12.79. The theatrical release for Alien (1979) was 6th December, 1979 (6.12.79 in the English date format). It is believed that Aliens (1986) is set in the year 2179, with Alien (1979) set 57 years earlier in 2122.

To most of the crew, the choice of James Cameron as director was mystifying as The Terminator (1984) hadn't been released at that stage. The film's assistant director continually questioned Cameron's decisions and was openly antagonistic towards him. Ultimately producer Gale Anne Hurd had no choice but to fire him and he briefly instigated a mass walk-out from the rest of the crew. Fortunately this was quickly resolved but caused some doubt as to whether the film would make it to completion.

Four actors from this movie appear in various Terminator movies: Michael Biehn, Lance Henriksen and Bill Paxton in The Terminator (1984), and Jenette Goldstein in Terminator 2: Judgment Day (1991).

During Hudson's (Bill Paxton) boasting monologue aboard the drop ship (special edition only) he talks about some of the weaponry of the Colonial Marines, mentioning a "phased plasma pulse rifle" - the pulse rifles the marines carry are ballistic, not "phased plasma", but the line references The Terminator (1984) (also directed by James Cameron, and featuring Paxton in a minor role) in which the terminator asks a gun store clerk for a "phased plasma rifle".

Hicks was originally played by James Remar, but Michael Biehn replaced him a few days after principal photography began, due to "artistic differences" between Remar and director James Cameron. However, Remar still appears in the finished film - but wearing the same armor, and shot from behind, it's impossible to tell the difference between the two actors.

The body mounts for Vasquez's and Drake's smart guns are taken from Steadicam gear.

In an interview, composer James Horner felt that James Cameron had given him so little time to write a musical score for the film, he was forced to cannibalize previous scores he had done, such as elements from his Star Trek II: The Wrath of Khan (1982) and Star Trek III: The Search for Spock (1984) scores, as well as adapt a rendition of "Gayane Ballet Suite" for the main and end titles. Horner stated that the tensions with Cameron were so high during post-production that he assumed they would never work together again. However, Cameron loved the score from Braveheart (1995) so much, the two mutually agreed that Horner would write the score for Titanic (1997), because it was a story they both wanted to do. They've let bygones be bygones ever since, especially when they won their Oscars for Titanic (1997) and collaborated again 12 years later for Avatar (2009).

Since production took place in England, the director
and producers conveniently cast many American actors
who were already living in England. This was
particularly important for the actress playing Newt,
who had to be a minor. Carrie Henn, who played Newt,
was an American girl living with her family in England
(actually, a bit of an English accent can be heard when
she says, "Let's go," and, "There is a short-cut across
the roof," during the Alien attack at the end of the
movie). Her movie brother Timmy (seen only in the
extended version) is also her real-life brother
Christopher Henn.

According to the shooting script, Vasquez and Drake
spent a tough childhood together in a Hispanic slum,
and were drafted into the Colonial Marines from
juvenile prison.

Michael Biehn got the call on a Friday night asking him
to take over the role of Hicks and was in London to
start filming on the following Monday.

Three different types of smoke were used in the film,
one of which has since become illegal to be used on
movie sets.

Ripley's miniature bathroom in her apartment is
actually a British Airways toilet, purchased from the
airline.

One of the perfect locations they found was a
decommissioned coal-fired power plant in Acton, West
London. The only trouble with it was that it was
heavily riddled with asbestos. So, a team was sent in
to clean up the plant, and atmosphere readings had to
be taken constantly throughout filming in this location
to make sure that the air was clear of contamination.
Ironically, the Acton location turned out to have
better atmospheric quality than Pinewood Studios.

When the set crews were looking around for floor
grating to use on the Sulaco set design, they asked a
local set design manufacturer/shop if they had anything
of the sort. Indeed they did, an immense pile of old
floor grating had been sitting out in the back of their

shop for the last seven years. It was left there from when they tore down the set of Alien (1979).

A Spydor toy from the He-Man franchise was bought as a reference to test how the facehuggers would move.

Armorer Terry English made three sets of armor for each member of the cast who needed to wear armor. He was only given two weeks to complete the job and upon arriving back at his workshop a few hours drive away from the film set, he realized he had forgotten the scrap of cloth James Cameron had given him so that the camouflage on the armor could be matched correctly to the uniforms the Marines would be wearing. Instead of going all the way back, English painted the completed sets of armor from memory.

The result was a pattern and color combination were not too dissimilar to the British Army DPM pattern. Fortunately, Cameron liked the contrast between the armor and the BDUs (Battle Dress Uniforms) the Marines wore beneath it, saying it makes the armor more obvious to the eye.

The graffiti you see on some of the armor was done by the actors themselves, with a little help from English for a few details like Hicks' clasp and padlock on his chest armor. The armor was hand made from Aluminum and all in one size, with on set adjustments made by English to make them fit each actor.

In the air shaft where Vasquez shoots the alien with a handgun, Jenette Goldstein could not handle the recoil of the gun properly. As a result, producer Gale Anne Hurd doubled for Vasquez in shots where the gun is fired. She was the only woman available who had experience firing handguns. Goldstein's flinching at the firing of a gun is also masked during the operations room fight immediately preceding the air shaft scene, when Vasquez is seen firing two grenades at the aliens - for the first one, there's a barely visible cut (Goldstein's head changes position suddenly) and for the second shot there is a smash-cut away
from her face at the moment of firing.

James Cameron was not impressed by the way that Ray Lovejoy was editing the film, and was seriously considering firing him and having the film re-edited from scratch by Mark Goldblatt, Cameron's editor on The Terminator (1984), and Peter Boita, who had already been bought on-board to edit the more dialogue driven scenes. Upon hearing that his job was in danger, Lovejoy grabbed all the footage from the film's final battle, locked himself in an editing suite over the weekend, and presented the fully edited version of the battle to Cameron the following week. Cameron was sufficiently impressed to let Lovejoy stay on-board and supervise what was intended to be the final edit.

Several references to Robert A. Heinlein's novel, "Starship Troopers": the prominent use of the military; during the orientation when Hudson asks if this is a "bug hunt."

Only six alien suits were used, and even then they were mostly just a handful of latex appliances on black leotards. The appearance of hundreds of aliens is simply clever editing and planning, and lighting plus slime helped make the "suits" more solid.

"Sulaco" is the name of the town in Joseph Conrad's "Nostromo".

All of the cast who were to play the Marines (with the exception of Michael Biehn, who replaced James Remar one week into filming) were trained by the S.A.S.

(Special Air Service, Britain's elite special operations unit) for two weeks before filming. Sigourney Weaver, Paul Reiser, and William Hope didn't participate/attend the training because director James Cameron felt it would help the actors create a sense of detachment between the three and the Marines - the characters these three actors played were all outsiders to the squad; Ripley being an advisor to the Marines while on the trip to LV-426, Burke being there just for financial reasons and Gorman being a newly-promoted Lieutenant with less experience than most of the Marines.

James Cameron had the actors (the Marines) personalize their own costumes (battle armor and fatigues) for added realism (much like soldiers in Vietnam wrote and drew things on their own helmets). Actress Cynthia Dale Scott, who plays Corporal Dietrich has the words "BLUE ANGEL" written on the back of her helmet, a reference to Marlene Dietrich in The Blue Angel (1930) or Blue Angel. Bill Paxton has "Louise" written on his armor. This is a dedication to his real-life wife, Louise Newbury.

While salary negotiations were going on with Sigourney Weaver to reprise her character in the second movie, the studio asked James Cameron to work on an alternative storyline excluding Ripley, but James Cameron indicated the series is all about Ripley and refused to do so.

Inside the APV preparing for battle, "El riesgo siempre vive!" can be seen scrawled in white across Vasquez's armor. Literally translated from Spanish this is: "Risk always lives!"; a variant of the Ancient Roman slogan "Luck favors the bold."

The Alien Queen has transparent teeth, as opposed to the warrior aliens.

Hudson says the word "man" a total of 35 times.

A lightweight dummy model of Newt (Carrie Henn) was constructed for Sigourney Weaver to carry around during the scenes just before the Queen chase.

Was voted the 42nd Greatest Film of all time by Entertainment Weekly. They describe it as the "greatest pure action movie ever."

Al Pacino visited the set as he was filming Revolution (1985) in the studio next door.

A complicated effect shot (the Marines entering the Alien nest) had already been filmed just before James Remar was replaced by Michael Biehn. A re-shoot would be too expensive, so the Corporal Hicks seen with his back towards camera is still played by James Remar.

When the crew is getting dressed after waking up from hypersleep, Hudson says, "Hey Vasquez, have you ever been mistaken for a man?" to which Vasquez answers, "No. Have you?" This is "borrowed" from a Hollywood legend involving columnist Earl Wilson and actress Tallulah Bankhead. He asked "Have you ever been mistaken for a man?" and she said, "No darling. Have you?"

The mechanism used to make the face-huggers thrash about in the stasis tubes in the science lab came from one of the "flying piranhas" in one of James Cameron's earlier movies Piranha Part Two: The Spawning (1981). It took nine people to make the face-hugger work: one person for each leg and one for the tail.

The portable computers used in the sentry gun scenes are GRiD GridCase 1535EXPs. Rugged and light due to their magnesium alloy enclosures, GRiD computers were used by the US military in combat and by NASA on early 1980s Space Shuttle missions.

Some of the sound effects for this film were created with help from the Fairlight, an early Australian-made digital sampler. Though the machine sampled at a now-laughable 8 bit resolution, the Fairlight then cost an astounding 30 thousand dollars (USD) and was state-of-the-art. Musicians such as Jan Hammer, Kate Bush, and Prince have used it extensively throughout their respective careers.

James Cameron married producer Gale Anne Hurd during production.

In the shooting script, the synthetic Ash from the previous movie was referred to as a 'Cyberdyne Systems 120-A/2', an obvious nod to the Cyberdyne Systems 101 Terminator from The Terminator (1984), James Cameron's previous movie. It was changed in the movie to a Hyperdine System 120-A2.

The title of Alien (1979) in Hungarian was "The 8th passenger: Death". Consequently, the title of Aliens (1986) was: "The name of the planet: Death".

The various screens and displays, seen mostly in the backgrounds, are actually TV screens with a video running. The film was shot in the UK where televisions run at 25 frames per second, however, film is normally shot and projected at 24 frames per second! Filming the TV monitors at that speed would cause the TV screens to run out of sync with the film, so they would have flickered terribly. Instead, the shots containing the monitors were taken at 25 frames per second to keep the monitors in sync, so when
these are then projected at the standard rate of 24 fps, they now run a bit slower than real-life.

Michael Biehn stated that he didn't get to customize his armor because he was cast so late in production. For the most part he liked all of the custom work on his, but he states that he hated the heart with the padlock on the chest plate as it was far too much like a bulls-eye.

A scene on the colony before the alien outbreak was deleted from the final cut. Elements of that scene show up in later James Cameron projects. The line, '... and we always get the same answer: 'Don't ask'.' was used in Terminator 2: Judgment Day (1991). In fact the entire scene in Terminator 2 follows the same pacing and tone as the scene cut from the theatrical version of Aliens: - an employee flags down a supervisor and they walk together, talking about the behavior of their employer - Weyland-Yutani in Aliens, CyberDyne Systems in Terminator 2 - and ending in the line '...don't ask.'. The character name 'Lydecker' was used in Dark Angel (2000).

The initial cinematographer was Dick Bush. However, director James Cameron fired him a month into production because he wasn't satisfied with the lighting, and the two men reportedly hated working with each other. Cameron then tried to hire Derek Vanlint, the DP on the previous film. Vanlint wasn't interested, but recommended Adrian Biddle for the job.

Stephen Lang auditioned for the role of Carter Burke. He would later play a villain in Avatar (2009), also directed by James Cameron.

The camo pattern worn by the Marines was custom made for the movie, but due to its similarity it is often confused for one called "frog and leaf," which is no longer in production.

James Horner wasn't particularly happy with the treatment of his score for the film despite receiving his first Oscar nomination. He delivered a finished score which didn't sit well with the edited film. Because Horner was unavailable as he was working on another film at the time, James Cameron had to heavily chop up the score to fit his edit. (A Deluxe Edition soundtrack of the score has since been released by Varèse Sarabande.)

The rhyme that Hudson mutters as he's searching for the colonists is from the AC/DC song "Shake a Leg": "Stop your grinnin' and drop your linen..."

Many of the characters in the movie whose first names are never mentioned, actually share their first name of the actor/actress portraying them:
e.g. Sgt. Al Apone (Al Matthews), Cpl. Collette Ferro (Colette Hiller), Pfc. Jenette Vasquez (Jenette Goldstein), Pvt. Mark Drake ('Mark Rolston (I)'), Pvt. Daniel Spunkmeyer (Daniel Kash), Pvt. Ricco Frost (Ricco Ross), Pvt. Trevor Wierzbowski (Trevor Steedman), and director Paul van Leuwen (Paul Maxwell).

Producers David Giler and Walter Hill were keen to work with James Cameron after having read his script for The Terminator (1984). Cameron went in for a meeting with the two producers and pitched several ideas at them, none of which they were that receptive to. As he was leaving, however, they did mention that they were thinking of doing a sequel to Alien (1979), and immediately Cameron's interest was piqued. Cameron submitted a 40-50 page treatment of what he would do for an "Alien" sequel which contained a lot of ideas for an existing treatment he had done for a script called "Mother". Giler and Hill loved Cameron's treatment and commissioned him to write a screenplay. Cameron got the good news the same day he landed screenwriting duties for Rambo: First Blood Part II (1985).

James Horner's schedule only allowed for him to work on the film for 6 weeks. He arrived in London to perform his duties, only to find that they were still shooting, much less editing. He sat around for 3 weeks before being able to get started.

Jenette Goldstein's character, Vasquez, inspired the character Tasha Yar on Star Trek: The Next Generation, and Goldstein herself was initially considered for the part. She later went on to make a brief appearance in Star Trek: Generations (1994). Bill Paxton's character, Hudson, inspired the character Guy Freeman in the Star Trek spoof Galaxy Quest (1999), which also starred Sigourney Weaver.

The M-56 smart guns and the sentry guns built for the movie were designed around German MG 42 machine guns (most recognizable on the smart guns where the MG 42's characteristic recoil booster muzzle is clearly visible). The gun is mounted on a heavily modified steadicam harness - the MG 42 alone (without the additional cosmetic dressing and ammunition) weighs in at about 25 pounds.

At one time during filming, the APC had an actual roof. But, during the "Fire In the hole" scene, the actors were actually suffocating from the fire's smoke. After a few tries, the roof of the APC was removed.

In the Court of Inquiry scene, all the chairs are automobile seats with the headrests removed. The circular holes at the top of each seat back are for the headrest posts.

James Cameron wrote the script two months before he left production to direct The Terminator (1984).

James Cameron had several designers come up with ideas for the drop ship that took the Marines from the Sulaco to the planet. Design after design, he finally gave up on them to come up with one he liked and constructed his own drop ship out of a model of an apache helicopter and other spare model pieces.

Bishop states that he can't harm a human. This is why he places his hand on top of Hicks' during the knife trick.There were two versions of the "Bug Stompers" logo designed for the movie, one wearing sneakers, and one wearing combat boots as seen on the drop ship.

The armor for the film was built by English armorer Terry English, and painted using Humbrol paints.

When Carter Burke and Marine Lieutenant Gorman are trying to convince Ripley to return to the colony, he mentions the Colony Marines are "Real tough hombres". "Tough 'Ombres" is an actual 90th infantry division from WWI and WWII. No need to add that "hombres" means "men" in Spanish, and "ombres" means "shadows" in French.

Sigourney Weaver threatened to not do any more "Alien" movies after seeing the movie's final cut, so as a compromise, the 1987 Special Edition was released on Laser-Disc.

The space station above earth is called Gateway, a possible reference to Frederik Pohl's "Gateway" novel, a sci-fi classic.

The pulse rifles that the Marines use are made from a Thompson M1A1 machine gun with a Remington 870 shotgun (shortened to just 15 inches and covered by the also-cut-down shroud and fore-grip from a Franchi SPAS 12 shotgun) underneath.

A set design company offered to build James Cameron a complete and working APC vehicle from scratch, but the cost was far too high for the budget he had in mind.The colony on LV-426 is named Hadley's Hope, with a population of 158. This is revealed in the special edition, and if you look carefully, the saying "Have A Nice Day" is painted on the sign.

The pistol used by Colonial Marines is a Heckler and Koch VP70.

United States Colonial Marines personnel service numbers:
SFC Apone, A A19/TQ4.0.32751E8
Pt Crowe, T A46/TQ1.0.98712E6
Cpl Dietrich, C A41/TQ8.0.81120E2
Pt Drake, M A23/TQ2.0.47619E7
Cpl Ferro, C A71/TQ9.0.09428E1
Pt Frost, R A17/TQ4.0.61247E5
Lt Gorman, S A09/TQ4.0.56124E3
Cpl Hicks, D A27/TQ4.0.48215E9
Pt Hudson, W A08/TQ1.0.41776E3
Pt Spunkmeyer, D A23/TQ6.0.92810E7
Pt Vasquez, J A03/TQ7.0.15618E4
Pt Wierzbowski, T A14/TQ8.0.20034E7

At the film's premiere, Paul Reiser's sister physically struck him because his character, Burke, was so contemptible.

Jenette Goldstein (Vasquez) actually did the chin-up curls and behind-the-head pull-ups, at the request of director James Cameron to establish Vasquez as the "tough" woman in the platoon.

The hip-mounted guns used by Vasquez and Drake were invented by James Cameron for the film. The props are based on steadicam movie camera rigs.

The full-size queen puppet was actually too big to fit into the elevator. For the shot where she is seen there, her tail was removed, and yet the back of the elevator still had to be opened to accommodate the prop; smoke effects, dark lighting, and a black curtain at the back to obscure the lack of tail.

The derelict model (seen in the extended edition) is the same model used in the first film. Fox had turned the model over to effects wizard (and prop archivist) Bob Burns, who had the prop sitting in his driveway. With some repair, it was able to be reused for the brief appearance in this film.

Most of the shots where it appears that the aliens are crawling quickly through tunnels or airducts were filmed using a vertical shaft with the camera at the bottom and the alien actor lowered headfirst on a cable.

In the original Alien (1979), one of the options
considered was making the creature translucent. Since
this wasn't done in the earlier movie, for continuity
it couldn't be used for the creatures in this film,
although it survives in one small way: the queen's
teeth are translucent.

The helmets the Marines wear are modified M-1 ballistic
helmets.

Sergeant Apone's full rank is listed as "SFC" on a
computer monitor. That is the abbreviation for the
current U.S. Army rank of Sergeant First Class, which
is usually a platoon sergeant position. The equivalent
current U.S. Marine Corps rank would be Gunnery
Sergeant, abbreviated GySgt. SFC Apone also wears the
current Army gold and green stripes of a Sergeant First
Class.

Sentry guns featured in special edition are of UA 571
model as viewed on their laptop management console.
Funny enough, Bill Paxton (pvt. Hudson) appeared as Lt.
Cmdr. Mike Dahlgren in submarine movie U-571 (2000).

When Burke and Ripley are discussing her psych
evaluation results, a People magazine can be seen on a
table.

Footage from this movie was used in a DirecTV
commercial.

The second of four Alien movies starring Sigourney
Weaver.

Aliens was the last of the series that Stan Winston
would do the alien effects on the special effects torch
would be given to two very innovative and design
legends of Alec Gillis and Tom Woodruff Jr.

In the MedLab scene there is a futuristic piece of
medical apparatus that can be briefly seen hanging from
the ceiling that has three objects hanging off of it.
These objects are actually three Generation One
Transformers toys, namely the Decepticon Shockwave. The
toys have been spray-painted a dull silver color and
are in their laser gun 'mode', but with each of the

Shockwave toy's arms (i.e. the laser gun's barrel) split apart. In this 'semi-transformation' the toy looks like a kind of futuristic grasping tool or perhaps even a laser scalpel.

Vic Armstrong says in his memoirs he was offered this film.

Paul Reiser subsequently appeared in Beverly Hills Cop II (1987) for director Tony Scott, whose brother Ridley Scott directed the original Alien (1979).

In an interview with Moviefone Sigourney Weaver said that each time one of the actors was to "die" she would give them a bouquet of flowers before filming began. When it was time for Paul Reiser to be killed she gave him a handful of dead blossoms.

Lance Henriksen caught a dose of food poisoning from the milk and yogurt combination that he had to spew up when his chest was pierced by the alien queen's tail. Having this lactose combination sitting around under hot studio lights created a bacterial breeding ground. Curiously, the crew of the first Alien (1979) film opted not to use milk for Ash's "death" scene (where he also spews the milky substance out
of his mouth) as they thought a fluid made of milk would go sour under the hot lights (see also trivia for Alien (1979)).

In the original script, when Ripley is rescuing Newt, she encounters a cocooned Burke (Paul Reiser) in the power plant. He claims he can feel the chestburster inside him and asks for help. Ripley gives him a live grenade and moves on. This scene was filmed and the only proof that it existed for decades was a single still image from a magazine. The scene was finally made available in full on the film's Blu-Ray release.

Although the first script draft turned in on 30 May 1985 was very close to the final film, some scenes in this version were dropped or changed in the final film, though most remained in Alan Dean Foster's novelization. Those include:
Ripley's nightmare was quite bloody, with a quick glimpse of the chestburster. Ripley and Burke waiting outside for the board's final decision; Ripley is convinced they think she is crazy. A longer scene with the Jordan family arguing; apparently, Newt and Timmy often play hide-and-seek inside the facility, which she calls 'Monster Maze'. A shower scene aboard the Sulaco. Ripley going into more detail about the facehuggers while briefing the Marines, calling the facehugger "a walking sex organ" to which Hudson replies, "Sounds like you, Hicks." While nearing LV-426, Gorman re-confirms that there is no communication whatsoever from the colony. There are thirty atmospheric processing units on the planet, as opposed to only one in the final film. The initial sweep of the colony complex includes the colonists' quarters as well. A dangling piece of ceiling sets off the motion tracker (white mice in the movie). Ripley returns into the APC, not yet ready to enter the complex. When she finally goes in, she is startled at the door by Pvt. Wierzbowski, who kept an eye on her. Gorman telling Burke that the Company can write off its share of the colony; Burke replies it is insured anyway. Ripley offers to be Newt's friend, but she declines, thinking Ripley will be dead soon anyway. Newt explains she evaded the Aliens because she was so good at playing Monster Maze. The resin from the Alien nest contains furniture, wires, as well as human bones. During the Alien attack, Apone hands back the rifle magazines, ignoring Gorman's order. During the escape, Gorman is stung unconscious by an Alien and almost pulled out of the APC; Hicks uses a gun turret to blast the Alien off the roof.

Burke stresses the importance of the Aliens more strongly, even offering Ripley a higher percentage if she cooperates. Newt formally offering Ripley to be her daughter; Ripley likes the idea. Bishop reveals that Gorman's catatonia is caused by a neuromuscular toxin from an Alien's stinger (replaced by the discovery that Alien blood gets neutralized through oxidation in the movie). Bishop also predicts that the Queen has a large abdomen, and possesses basic intelligence. After the first sentry gun attack, a motion sensor indicates the Aliens have breached the door, and have entered the complex. Bishop encountering an Alien while crawling along the tunnel (this scene also appeared in the final script but neither in the theatrical release nor in the Special Edition). Gorman asks Vasquez if she still wants to kill him; she replies it won't be necessary. The second drop ship refueling itself before leaving the Sulaco under Bishop's remote control. Hicks uses a welder to open a duct into a service way. From there, Newt falls into a chute. Ripley follows, but takes a different chute.

The first draft also included a scene with a cocooned Burke, which was shot but not included in any of the versions of the movie.

There are tiny albino versions of the warrior Aliens in the egg chamber, which pick up the eggs.

Sigourney Weaver told James Cameron that she wanted to do three things in the movie; not handle a weapon, die, and make love to an alien. While none of these wishes were fulfilled, she got to do all three in Alien[3] (1992) - second and third - and Alien: Resurrection (1997) in which she fought aliens just physically.

According to the 1991 Special Widescreen Collector's Edition Laserdisc release of the movie (presented on the Bonus Disc of the 2003 Alien Quadrilogy DVD Box Set), James Cameron turned in the first treatment for the film, called "Alien II" at the time, on 21 September 1983. Some of the differences between this initial treatment and the final film included the following: - The character of Carter Burke was absent, instead, his dialogue was given to someone named Dr. O'Niel, who did not join Ripley and the marines on their voyage to the colony planet. - Instead of being taken to the Gateway Station, Ripley was taken to Earth Station Beta. - The name of the colony planet was Acheron, taken from the script of Alien (1979), instead of LV-426. - Ripley's daughter was alive, and Ripley had a disheartening videophone conversation with her, where she blamed Ripley for abandoning her by going to space. - There were multiple atmospheric processors on the planet. - The initial discovery of the aliens on the colony planet is much longer, where it is shown how Newt's father gets to the site of the eggs and is jumped by a facehugger. - An additional scene involves a rescue team going to the site of the alien eggs and being jumped by tens of facehuggers.
- The aliens sting people to paralyze them before either killing or cocooning them. - At one point Ripley, Newt and Hicks get cocooned. - The aliens cocooning people are a different breed. They look like smaller, albino versions of the warrior aliens. - Bishop refuses to land on the planet and pick up Ripley, Hicks and Newt, indicating "the risk of contaminating other inhabited worlds is too great." - Ripley ends up using the colonists' shuttle to get back to the Sulaco. - Bishop tells her: "You were right about me all along."

The first draft script was turned in by Cameron on 30 May 1985. This draft was quite different from the treatment, but very close to the final film.

The music that plays when the Alien Queen appears as Ripley and Newt wait for the elevator is a reused piece from Jerry Goldsmith's score for the original Alien (1979).

Thematically, the music appears in both movies at the same time: near the end, as Ripley tries to escape from an alien while the environment around her counts down to self-destruction (the Nostromo in Alien (1979), and the atmosphere processor in Aliens (1986)).

The pouch Ripley takes onto the lift at the end of the movie is a British Armed Forces respirator haversack.

At the very end of the credits the sound of an Alien egg can be heard opening

Alien³ (1992)
 114 min - Action | Sci-Fi | Thriller - 22 May 1992
(USA)

Ripley continues to be stalked by a savage alien, after
her escape pod crashes on a prison planet.

Director: David Fincher
Writers: Dan O'Bannon (characters), Ronald Shusett
(characters)
Stars: Sigourney Weaver, Charles S. Dutton, Charles
Dance

-A Couple Of Average Joe's
In trying to copy the original tension of the single
alien intruder, this films slows things down and fails
on almost every level. One of the biggest insults, is
the killing off of characters that we had come to love
from the previous films, negating all of Ripley's
efforts to save them. Ripley's held back by her
character being sick the entire film, as she deals with
a group of boring, religious convicts. The worst insult
comes at the films climax with a stretched out death
scene that tries to be more poignant than it really is.
Director David Fincher even tried to get his name
removed from this depressing movie.

First-time director David Fincher disowned the film,
citing constant studio interference and actually walked
out of production before final editing began. He did
preside over a rough cut that became the basis for the
'Assembly Cut', a longer version of the movie later
released on DVD and Blu-ray.

One possible idea for the film included a chest-burster
coming out of Michael Biehn's character, Hicks. A
replica of the actor with his chest torn open was
created, but after Biehn discovered this, he threatened
to sue the producers for using his likeness without his
consent, and the idea was dropped. Later, the producers
paid him to use his picture at the beginning of the
film for the computer sequence. Apparently he received
more money for use of this one image than for his role
in Aliens (1986).

$7 million had been spent on sets that were never used thanks to the ever-changing script before filming had even started.

At one point, David Fincher was denied permission by the film's producers to shoot a crucial scene in the prison understructure between Ripley and the alien. Against orders, Fincher grabbed Sigourney Weaver, a camera and shot the scene anyway. This scene appears in the final cut.

Original Alien (1979) Director Ridley Scott turned down the chance to direct. Scott, and later Renny Harlin both thought the third film should explore the origin of the Xenomorph species. This concept was deemed too expensive by David Giler and Walter Hill, so Scott declined to return and Harlin later quit the film. Scott ultimately got his wish with the movie Prometheus (2012).

William Gibson wrote a very early script treatment for the film, which was initially intended as a two-parter to be shot back-to-back. As Sigourney Weaver's involvement was in question, the main focus of this script was between Hicks and Bishop, two characters from Aliens (1986). Many consider this to be a much superior script. The only carry-over from this original script, however, is the bar-codes on the back of the convicts' necks.

With the release of the definitive Alien Quadrilogy on DVD in 2004, 20th Century Fox proffered David Fincher the proverbial olive branch and asked him to assemble and comment on his own Director's Cut. Fincher declined. He was the only one of the four Alien directors to refuse to have anything to do with the project.

Cinematographer Alex Thomson replaced Jordan Cronenweth after only two weeks of filming, after he began to suffer the onset of Parkinson's Disease. Though Cronenweth insisted that he was well enough to make it until the end of production, and David Fincher supported him, line producer Ezra Swerdlow forced Cronenweth off the film, largely because he had lost his own father to the same illness several years previously and knew that if anything, the demanding schedule would likely take a fatal toll on Cronenweth's health.

Off-duty, Sigourney Weaver had to wear a wig as her then two-year-old daughter Charlotte didn't like to see her mother bald.

Because of continuing troubles with the film, Fox halted production in Pinewood Studios in England in late 1991. The crew returned to LA, and an initial screening identified the missing parts of the film. A major part yet to be shot included killing of the alien in the lead pool. By the time of the new shots in LA, Sigourney Weaver's hair grew back, and she had an agreement with the producers that if she would have to cut her hair she would be paid a $40,000 bonus. The producers therefore hired Greg Cannom to create a bald cap with very short hair on it. The make-up process cost $16,000 and was very difficult and time-consuming because the hairline required the cap to be placed very precisely on Weaver's head.

Lance Henriksen only agreed to reprise his role as Bishop as a personal favor to Walter Hill. To this day, Henriksen has said he dislikes the film for its nihilistic themes.

One early draft of the script focused almost entirely on Hicks, Bishop and Newt, played in Aliens (1986) by Michael Biehn, Lance Henriksen and Carrie Henn respectively. The story would tie up loose ends from the preceding film with Newt returning to Earth to live with her grandparents, as well as Hicks and Bishop and a new team of Colonial Marines battling a rival faction of planets who use the Alien as a bio-weapon. The latter was used somewhat in Aliens: Colonial Marines (2013)

When David Fincher asked Sigourney Weaver how she felt about going bald for the role, she jokingly replied "Its fine with me only as long as I get more money!"

The crane that lifts the crashed EEV out of the water to dry land is a miniature built using the cannibalized parts from a Star Wars X-Wing fighter model kit.

Dr. Clemens' line about Fury-161 being one of 'Weyland-Yutani's backwater prison planets.' was the first time the name Weyland-Yutani was spoken out loud. It had appeared on computer screens and props in the previous two films, Alien (1979) and Aliens (1986), but characters always referred to it as 'The Company' in dialogue.

The film spent over a year in editing.

Although the alien that hatched from the dog was a rod puppet, early filmed tests used an actual dog in an alien costume.

An advanced type of facehugger, one that impregnates Ripley with a queen embryo, was designed and built, but was cut from the Theatrical Version. It does however make a brief appearance in the extended Assembly Cut.

The original budget was $45 million which included
Sigourney Weaver's fee of $5.5 million. The budget soon
spiraled however, with first Renny Harlin and then
Vincent Ward both leaving the project before novice
feature film director David Fincher came on board.
Extensive last minute re-shoots - especially after the
finale was deemed to be too similar to Terminator 2:
Judgment Day (1991) - ultimately pushed the budget into
the region of $65 million.

Much more of the autopsy scene was filmed than ended up
in the final film. A rough cut of the scene originally
contained so much gore, that it even made crew members
who had worked on it sick to their stomach.

Writer/Producer David Giler has stated he regrets
writing this movie, as it eroded his authority as
producer. Giler only committed to writing the film upon
demands from Sigourney Weaver who, after Vincent Ward's
departure, would only sign on to the film if Giler and
Walter Hill would pen the screenplay. Giler claims this
later generated conflicts between himself, director
David Fincher and Fox Studios executives, with Fox
taking Fincher's side over Giler's.

After one particularly heated disagreement, Giler
walked off the set, leaving his duties to producer John
Landau.

David Twohy contributed to the pile of abandoned
scripts the movie's pre-production generated. In his
version, the only returning character is Ripley, who
only briefly appears on a file card. As in previous
scripts the story involves experiments in genetically-
engineering aliens as bioweapons. This script
introduced a high-security prison facility in space and
its morally ambiguous inmates (one of which is an
escape artist), themes which made it into both the
finished product, and Twohy's own Pitch Black (2000).

Costume Designer Bob Ringwood walked off the film early
in production after finding Director David Fincher
difficult and unpleasant to work with.

David Twohy, Vincent Ward, John Fasano, Renny Harlin,
David Fincher, Larry Ferguson, David Giler and Walter

Hill all attempted to claim credit for the screenplay during the arbitration process. Four more writers could have claimed credit but chose not to; William Gibson and Eric Red saw no point in doing so the film had changed substantially from their early drafts, Greg Pruss was talked out of claiming credit in exchange for guaranteed work elsewhere, and Rex Pickett, despite having written a substantial amount of the shooting script, declined to seek credit due to how unpleasant his experience of working on the film had been.

Because an early storyline of the movie involved aliens landing on Earth, an early trailer of the movie had the tagline "On Earth, everyone can hear you scream."

The Rottweiler (from which the alien emerges) had to have part of his face shaved to indicate where the facehugger had gripped onto him.

The creature that the alien impregnates was originally an ox, but was eventually changed because an ox was cumbersome and was seen as somewhat incongruous when placed in the film's environment. This sequence was later restored for the extended "Assembly Cut."

Sigourney Weaver had a clause in her contract specifying that Walter Hill and David Giler would write the final shooting script. Weaver has said that she considers Ripley a very difficult character to write, and, with the exception of James Cameron, only Giler and Hill have really ever written the character correctly.

Novelist Alan Dean Foster who wrote the novelization of the film objected to the storyline, most specifically, the deaths of Newt and Hicks. His initial draft of the novel had Newt survive but the studio rejected this, forcing Foster to keep his adaptation consistent with the film. For this reason, the author declined to write any other adaptation of the franchise.

The alien in this movie differs from its predecessors in that the organic pipes on its back are now missing and it now has a more pronounced set of lips.

There are screenplay treatments by Eric Red, David Twohy, John Fasano and Rex Pickett all freely available on the Internet.

The damages inflicted on Bishop were too severe to have Lance Henriksen work a prosthetic head while hiding under a table/chair/platform, so the filmmakers ended up having the android being played by... an android. A mechanical copy of Henriksen's likeness was used in this movie for the portrayal of the Sulaco-Bishop.

Multiple proposed scripts caused misleading advertising which implied that the movie would be set on Earth. William Gibson also drafted a script in which Ripley spent most of the film in a coma.

On the set at Pinewood Studios, a giant lead foundry took 12 weeks to construct and put the production way behind. Even with 6 day weeks and 14 hour days, the crew were unable to keep up with the schedule.

The same "dipping bird" appears on the warden's desk as was seen in the original Alien (1979).

Gabriel Byrne was offered the role of Clemens.

A cross is briefly seen on the planet surface to suggest the religion that some of the inmates have turned to. The model department held a competition to see who could design the best one. Four different models were created, and then David Fincher chose the version he liked best.

When Ripley retrieves Bishop from the trash heap and re-activates him to find out what happened on the Sulaco, she asks him, "Was there an alien on board?" This is the only time in the entire "Alien" franchise (including the "AvP" films) where the term "alien" is used to describe the creature. Everyone else uses other names (baddies, dragon, serpent, creature, xenomorph, animals, bug) to identify it.

This film is believed to be set just days or weeks after the events in Aliens (1986), in 2179.

Some of H.R. Giger's design for the film involved a puma-like alien with claws. The producers also instructed him to do more sexy designs, so he created a drawing of an alien, which, in close view, had the lips of a woman. One of his ideas involved the alien kissing the victims and killing them that way (an idea that was later used in the movie Species (1995) where the main creature was also designed by Giger).

The concept by Vincent Ward based on which the movie
was green-lighted involved an artificially constructed
wooden planetoid and a group of monks who thought they
were living in post-apocalyptic dark ages, and had a
middle-ages lifestyle. The group refused all kinds of
modern technology, and when Ripley and the Alien crash-
land on it, they would blame Ripley for the Alien
attacks. Ripley was to be impregnated by the Alien "the
old-fashioned way" rather than through a face-hugger,
and therefore being impregnated with a human-alien
hybrid. According to the storyboards, she would dream
of half human-half Alien hybrids. Other storyboards
included horse-Alien and sheep-Alien hybrids. The film
was to end with one of the monks performing an
'exorcism' on the Ripley, transferring the Alien embryo
to his own body, and then killing it by walking into a
fire. Ward left the project after the producers
insisted that he change the monks to prisoners and drop
the wooden planet idea. However, since many of Ward's
ideas were carried over to the final screenplay, it
still earned him a story credit.

To create a convincing corpse of the character of Newt,
the filmmakers created life size mannequins using the
molds of Carrie Henn from Aliens (1986).

The production effectively shut down for three months
while the script was undergoing rewrites.

When the powers-that-be decided on a new ending to be
shot, Elliot Goldenthal had one night to come up with a
new score.

The miniature of the coastline, seen when the EEV is
plummeting towards the planet, was given a sickly green
hue, to suggest that the area was polluted from decades
of industrial spilling.

Much like first Alien movie, Alien 3 also had problems
with negative reactions of audience who saw rough cut
of the movie in early test screenings and were
horrified from all the scenes of gore and violence.
Because of this and also to avoid NC-17 rating by MPAA,
Alien 3 was heavily cut.

Some of the graphic scenes that were deleted from rough
cut which is said to be 3 hours long include; Longer
and more disturbing version of Newt's autopsy scene,
close ups of melted face of prisoner who gets hit with
Alien's acid and some gore was cut from scene where he
falls into giant fan, bloodier version of Clemens'
death scene and some parts from final chase and fight
between prisoners and Alien.

This is the only film in the Alien Quadrilogy that does
not feature an android character unique to that film.
The only android that appears is Bishop (in a severely
damaged state), and he had previously appeared in the
film prior to this.

A series of Aliens comic books were published that were
set after the events in Aliens (1986), featuring an
adult Newt returning to space with a shell-shocked
Hicks to stop the retrieval of an alien specimen by
Weyland-Yutani corporation. The books were re-published
to accommodate Alien³ (1992), with Newt re-named Billy.

In the original drafts of the script there was no
Ripley.

In wide shots, most of the refinery is actually made of
cardboard.

Initially Renny Harlin was attached as director, but
left to direct Die Hard 2 (1990). Then Vincent Ward
came on board, but only lasted a few months before
being fired after several disagreements with the
producers. The scriptwriter, Walter Hill, was
considered to direct the film as well, but he stepped
back after David Fincher became available.

To create some of the wet sounds that accompany the alien, the soundmen went to Asian markets and bought animal heads and stomach linings.

There was some question mark over whether the character of Ripley should actually feature in this film until the then president of 20th Century Fox, Joe Roth, insisted otherwise.

Early versions of the script and design featured a giant rustic monastery. Also, the alien itself would not be appearing.

After the first draft was complete (in which the Alien attacks a monastery), construction work began on the sets. The construction shut down, leaving the crew in limbo, as the script was reworked. Although the location changed to a prison, it was decided that they would use the already half-built monastery sets.

Including the extended and director's cuts of each movie in the series, this is the only Alien film not to feature the cocoons.

Hungarian title translated back to English: "Final Solution: Death."

This is the only film in the Alien franchise that is actually a "numbered" sequel.

Richard E. Grant turned down the role of Clemens. Director David Fincher offered him the role as he was a huge fan of Withnail & I (1987) and wanted to reunite Grant with co-stars Paul McGann and Ralph Brown.

Apart from an occasional comment or order, doctor Clemens (Charles Dance) only talks with either Andrews (Brian Glover), Aaron (Ralph Brown) or Ripley (Sigourney Weaver) during the entire movie.

The tea glass that prison superintendent Andrews is sipping on is part of the BODUM series, a tableware manufactured in Denmark.

In the scene where the warden is addressing the prisoners regarding the deaths of the other prisoners, right after Ripley bursts in to warn them of the Alien and the Warden orders her removal, when the Alien yanks the Warden into the ceiling, you can see that one of the prisoners is wearing a Weyland-Yutani Corporation jacket, the logo is emblazoned on the back.

Vincent Ward used his pay off from this film to finance his next, Map of the Human Heart (1992).

Ralph Brown (Aaron) and Charles Dance (Clemens) were reunited in the 2007 movie "The Contractor", starring Wesley Snipes.

Alien 3 marks the first time a chestburster appears almost fully formed, instead of the pupa appearance of the previous installments. The chestburster looked like a scaled down version of the adult. This would later be seen in Prometheus, where "The Deacon" was born already fully formed.

When the movie was turned into a novel by Alan Dean Foster, writer of the novels of Alien and Aliens, an original draft of the novel had Ripley survive at the end, as he disliked the ending of the film. However, studio executives told him to remain true to the original ending. He changed his novel, which upset him so much, he refused an offer to write the Alien: Resurrection novelization. Instead, that book was written by A.C. Crispin.

The third of four Alien movies starring Sigourney
Weaver.

This is the first time Slow Motion cameras were used
intentionally in an Alien movie, seen when explosives
are being set, and one falls. The use of the cameras,
which were primitive at the time, resulted in a
squashed and blurred image, and stands out against the
normal speed recordings. The technique was then later
used briefly in the spin off, Prometheus.

The final shooting script, the novelization and the
comics adaptation confirm that Newt was the first one
to be facehugged. This is merely hinted during the
opening credits since the facehugger attacks and cracks
Newt's cryotube. When the scanner shows the facehugger
attached to a person, Ripley is shown in a seizure
state but she is clearly in her intact tube. After the
EEV crashlanded Newt drowned. She was sadly conscious
and cried for help. After she died the alien embryo
crawled out of her mouth and proceeded to Ripley's
chamber since it requires a living host to grow
properly. It opened Ripley's mouth and forced itself
into her throat. Although the scenes were storyboarded
they were never filmed because the effect of the
creature switching hosts could not be portrayed
realistically. The Theatrical Cut adds more confusion
to the backstory since the inmates discover Ripley
perfectly clean in her tube meaning that her capsule
was never violated. The Extended Cut however shows
Clemens discovering a half-drowned Ripley in the shore
covered in dirt and lice, meaning that she was already
out of her cryotube. This also accounts for the
continuity error in the theatrical cut since Ripley is
spotless in the EEV but she is dirty when Clemens
carries her in the infirmary.

The script went through so many rewrites and the film
was slated to be helmed by so many different directors
that when David Fincher came on board he stated that
the egg on Sulako was just a plot device to propel the
story of the film and there was never any intention of
explaining its presence. There is a lot of controversy
about how the egg was found on the Sulako. Some very
early drafts of the script however reveal that Bishop's

milky fluid was combined with the Queen's acid after
the sting and produced a new egg. This mirrors the
Director's Cut of Alien where Ripley finds the nest
with a cocooned Brett. The alien had covered him with
its fluid in order to transform him into a new egg and
Dallas was kept as a potential host for the facehugger.
This backstory was finally deleted because of the
various drafts the screenplay went through but it
provides a viable explanation as to why the egg did not
hatch immediately. It took a few days until the egg was
fully formed and then it opened when the facehugger
sensed living hosts in the cryogenic compartment.

Although this is one of the last big science-fiction
movies to use mostly traditional special effect
techniques (miniatures, animatronics and optical visual
effects), there is one notable effects shot that was
computer-generated: the head of the Alien cracking
after it has been cooled with water. Other uses of
computer-generated graphics include minor details, such
as added shadows and debris particles.

Near the end, Dillon sarcastically calls Morse (Danny
Webb) 'the guy who made a deal with God to live
forever'. Morse is indeed the only prisoner to survive
at the end.

Special Effects company Amalgamated Dynamics built a
special puppet of the queen alien for a sequence cut
from the film. Originally, the queen alien was supposed
to gestate in Newt until the EEV crash, when it would
swim out through the mouth of Newt's dead body and
embed itself in Ripley. This accounts for the confusing
sequence at the film's opening when the facehugger is
seen attacking Newt's cryotube, not Ripley's, which
only cracks during the actual ejection sequence. Though
not in the final film, this scene does appear in the
comic book adaptation.

Michael Behin had stated in an interview that he was deeply hurt that his character from "Aliens" Corporal Duane Hicks was killed off, after escaping with Ripley, Newt and Bishop at the end of the previous film and did not understand why Hicks had to be killed off.

The early scenes in the shooting script explain why Ripley has a sore throat and coughs continually during the film; the alien embryo had forced itself into her larynx violently.

Rex Pickett wrote the draft before David Giler and Walter Hill turned in their final shooting script. Pickett's screenplay keeps the former prisoners more faithful to their convictions since they never curse or use bad language. In the scene where Ripley conducts a cat scan the screenplay by Rex Pickett clarifies that the larva is a distinctively visible queen because there are tiny white spots which are the future eggs. This explains how Ripley knew that she was carrying a queen embryo. The Company also knew this vital information since the catscanner data are transferred to their mainframe.

The company name written in Japanese can be briefly seen on the black box as Ripley retrieves it and on a poster in the office where 85 and Ripley contact the company for the second time. In a scene towards the end of the movie where Ripley and the inmates discuss the killing of the alien, several Kanji characters can be seen on the wall: "Chô-kô'on kiken" (danger: extremely high heat). The scrap yard where Bishop is discarded also displays a large red "tetsu" (iron).

One of the reasons for Newt being killed off, the Fiorina 161 prison planet has convicted child molesters, which would had resulted in an attempted child molestation scene, which the child molester convicts attempted to rape Newt. Instead, the rapist convicts try to rape Ripley.

Morse; the only survivor, has one line less than 10 minutes into the film. He isn't seen again until the Alien kills Andrews at the hour and 10 minute mark. (assembly cut runtime)

Alien: Resurrection (1997)
 109 min - Action | Sci-Fi | Thriller - 26 November
1997 (USA)

200 years after her death, Ellen Ripley is revived as a
powerful human/Alien hybrid clone who must continue her
war against the Aliens.

Director: Jean-Pierre Jeunet
Writers: Dan O'Bannon (characters), Ronald Shusett
(characters)
Stars: Sigourney Weaver, Winona Ryder, Dominique Pinon

-A Couple Of Average Joe's
Trying to remove the bad taste of Alien 3 from the it's
mouth, this film brings back Ripley from the dead via a
petrie dish as an amnesiac. She's cooler, tougher, and
a tremendous basketball player. The cast (particularly
Winona Ryder and Ron Perlman) add flavor to this fun
sequel. Well, it's fun until the idiotic human/alien
hybrid ending. Not bad but, ultimately unnecessary.

Sigourney Weaver made the behind-the-back half-court
basketball shot successfully after two weeks of
basketball practice, tutored by a basketball coach. Her
conversion rate during that two weeks was about one
shot in from every six. When the day came to shoot the
scene, director Jean-Pierre Jeunet wanted to have the
ball dropped in from above, rather than wait for Weaver
to sink the shot herself, which "would probably take
about 200 takes". Weaver insisted that the she could
get the shot in herself, which she was finally allowed
to do. She sunk the shot on the very first take, even
though she was six feet further past the three-point
line. Ron Perlman was completely stunned (and
thoroughly impressed), and turned directly at the
camera and broke character, saying, "Oh my God!" The
editors looked at the shot and decided that there was
"enough room to get the scissors in". Weaver was
excited about making the shot, but Jeunet was concerned
that audiences would believe the shot to be faked due
to the ball leaving the frame. Upon Weaver's
insistence, he kept the shot as it was. Weaver
described the miracle shot
as "one of the best moments in her life", after her
wedding day and the birth of her daughter, of course.

The opening shot of Ripley cloned, albeit as a young girl, was based on photographs that Sigourney Weaver had given the special effects crew of herself as a child.

When pre-production was underway, the original 'Alien Queen' could not be located and the molds that were used to build the original were damaged beyond usefulness.

Fortunately, the original life-size puppet was located in the personal collection of an avid Alien (1979) fan.

The underwater sequence marked the first time that Winona Ryder had gone underwater since a near-drowning incident that happened to her when she was 12 years old. The actress suffered a complete anxiety attack on the first day of filming in the underwater set.

Ron Perlman did most of his own stunts, particularly the scene in where he hangs upside down off a ladder by his legs whilst firing two guns at an alien. The next day, when he went to take a shower, he discovered that he had severely lacerated the backs of his knees in doing so.

Sigourney Weaver signed on to the film largely because of one scene in particular - when Ripley 8 encounters her previous 7 aborted genetic incarnations.

Joss Whedon has commented on his dissatisfaction with the movie. Fans had speculated that the finished article deviated from his original script in some fatal manner, however he put such rumors to rest. His dialogue, action and plot were essentially intact. However he had written with a playful, tongue-in-cheek tone, which didn't work when the director decided to "play it straight".

Eventually the Betty and her crew became the prototypes for Whedon's Firefly (2002), which captured the tone he had aimed for in this movie.

Actor Ron Perlman nearly drowned while filming the underwater sequence. At one point, when trying to surface, he hit his head on a sprinkler in the ceiling, knocking him out cold. He was rescued by nearby film crew members.

In her initial scenes with the Newborn, Sigourney Weaver makes a point of not looking in its eyes. This was a lesson learned from when she made Gorillas in the Mist (1988) in not making initial eye contact with a potentially dangerous animal.

Jean-Pierre Jeunet wanted to have a scene where a mosquito stings Ripley, then vanishes into smoke because of her acid blood. Eventually, he dropped the idea after the SFX team told him how much it would cost.

The studio wanted to cut the scene preceding Ripley's encounter with the alien queen because of its rather sexual nature. They decided to keep it when Sigourney Weaver threatened to not promote the film if the scene was cut.

The original idea for the movie was for Newt (the child from Aliens (1986)) to be cloned, not Ripley. This was changed when Sigourney Weaver agreed to reprise her role for $11 million.

Joss Whedon was unhappy with everything about the film. He later commented in 2005: "It wasn't a question of doing everything differently, although they changed the ending; it was mostly a matter of doing everything

wrong. They said the lines but they said them all
wrong. And they cast it wrong. And they designed it
wrong. And they scored it wrong. They did everything
wrong they could possibly do. That's actually a
fascinating lesson in filmmaking. Because everything
they did reflects back to the script or looks like
something from it. And people assume that if I hated it
then they'd changed the script...but it wasn't so much
they changed it, they executed it in such a ghastly
fashion they rendered it unwatchable.

The full-size Newborn animatronic puppet was originally
filmed with genitals that were a mix between male and
female genitals. They had to be digitally removed on
studio orders.

In the scene where Dominique Pinon appears out of an
elevator, his line originally was "Who were you
expecting? The Easter Bunny?" However, Pinon kept
saying "Eastern Bunny", to which his fellow actors
would break out in laughter. The crew later even
printed T-shirts with this line. Interestingly enough,
the new line "Who were you expecting, Santa Claus?" had
also been used in Jean-Pierre Jeunet's previous movie,
The City of Lost Children (1995), where it was directed
at Ron Perlman as well.

Winona Ryder agreed to do this film even before reading
the script. She stated that she "didn't care if she
died in the first scene", she'd do it. Ryder claimed
that then she could boast about being in an "Alien"
movie to her younger brothers.

This is the only Alien movie not to be shot in the
United Kingdom. One of the reasons for this was that
co-producer Sigourney Weaver didn't want to travel.

In order to heighten contrasts, cinematographer Darius Khondji added silver to the printing process. This had the result of making the dark colors richer and giving everything else a metallic tinge. He also used an electric blue tint for the underwater sequence.

Director Jean-Pierre Jeunet spoke almost no English at the time of shooting and had translators on set at all times. By the time the Special Edition DVD was released in 2003, he had learned enough English to record a director's commentary.

On the February 14, 2013 episode of Conan, William H. Macy revealed that the last time he'd done an audition was for the role of Dr. Gediman. During the audition with director Jean-Pierre Jeunet, he felt the scene he was reading was so ridiculous, he said "You know what guys, This is never going to happen," got up and left the room.

Sigourney Weaver was paid $11 million to come back as Ripley, which was the entire budget of Alien (1979) (not adjusted for inflation).

H.R. Giger was openly displeased that he wasn't given a credit for his alien designs and fired off a letter of protest to 20th Century Fox.

Milk had to be added to the underwater set as the water was simply too transparent to be convincing.

The production had trouble finding enough studio space as major productions like Titanic (1997), Starship Troopers (1997) and The Lost World: Jurassic Park (1997) were all taking up most of the available studio space in Hollywood.

Joss Whedon originally scripted the Newborn creature as a deadly four-legged, eyeless, bone-white creature with red veins running along the sides of its head. It had an inner jaw, similar to the all the other aliens. It also had a pair of pincers on the sides of his head. These pincers were used to hold its prey still as it drained the prey of blood with its inner jaw. The creature was also larger, nearly the size of the queen alien. In later script revisions, the creature was

changed into a "more believable" hybrid of human and
alien.

The $50-60 million budget was significantly lower than
the director and writers originally imagined.
Therefore, sets were toned down in scale and a more
claustrophobic shooting approach with a lot of close-
ups to characters' faces was taken.

Joss Whedon went through five different versions of the
final battle with the "Newborn" creature, the first
four versions of which all took place on Earth in such
settings as a hospital maternity ward, a giant
junkyard, a snowy forest and cliffside, and a desert.

The character of Dr. Wren was originally written for
Bill Murray, with the intent of reuniting him with
Sigourney Weaver, his co-star from Ghostbusters (1984).

Angelina Jolie turned down the role of Call.

Although it appears that the cast spend most of the
time wandering up and down endless spaceship corridors,
in reality there were only two built for the film.

As the film progresses, the walls of the ship's
corridors become darker and more ominous.

The underwater segment was shot on a specially constructed sound stage on the Fox lot, which was converted into a permanent water-tank. It took nearly a week to fill it with water.

The actors were subjected to about 15 underwater training sessions in swimming pools around the Los Angeles area before arriving at the underwater set where they underwent a further 2 weeks of training before anything was shot.

Sigourney Weaver missed most of this because she had been appearing in a play on Broadway just prior to filming.

The Auriga interactive computer is named "Father." In the original Alien (1979), the computer's name was "Mother." There are even compatible scenes where people yell at Mother or Father for not responding to them.

Takes place in 2379, 200 years after "Aliens" and "Alien 3" (2179) and also takes place 257 years after "Alien" (2122).

The Newborn was specifically given eyes to answer some of the criticism that had been made earlier about how the alien could actually see, as it had no apparent eyes.

The underwater scenes took three weeks to film.

Originally, the fourth alien movie was to be a rendition of the popular comic Aliens Vs. Predator, which combined the Alien creatures with Predator (1987) since 1991. It took another 7 years before AVP: Alien vs. Predator (2004) saw the light.

David Cronenberg was also an early choice to direct but later passed.

Jean-Pierre Jeunet wanted to shoot additional action scenes using a fully digital Newborn creature. He wanted Ripley to be chased by the Newborn in the escape from the Betty scene, but could not realize it due to budget constraints. In the final film, a full-size Newborn creature can be seen in only one scene and almost all of the scenes involving the creature are animatronic.

One of the concept designs of the Newborn involved the creature sporting a likeness of Sigourney Weaver's face.

This was abandoned as it bore too much of a similarity to Sil, the alien creature in Species (1995).

Winona Ryder was a big fan of Alien (1979) and jumped at the chance of appearing alongside her icon, Sigourney Weaver, for that reason.

WILHELM SCREAM: A soldier in the last escape pod when the alien enters it, right before Perez asks for the grenade.

In the theatrical release, H.R. Giger is not credited for his part in the design of the Aliens. The video release has his name in the closing credits.

Director Pierre Jeunet was given license to change the
script as much as he wanted, and the final film is
substantially different than Joss Whedon's original
script. Characters and situations were merged,
simplified or removed, and the overall tone was made
more fanciful and less realistic. Things changed or
removed include: An Asian assassin called St. Just
(pronounced "San-Jhoost") was original part of the
Betty's crew. Johner was described as being more of a
crazy, psychopathic character. After the underwater
sequence, the characters were then forced to climb up a
50 story lift-shaft, with aliens attacking them. After
the Chapel scene, there was an action sequence in the
ship's "farm", including a moment were the crew
discovers the army has been growing cannabis. The
Newborn alien was originally extremely deadly, the size
of a Queen alien, and there was little emotional
connection between it and Ripley. The final action
sequence took place on Earth, ending with the surviving
characters (including Ripley) deciding to stick
together.

To play Ripley 7, Sigourney Weaver stuck her head up
through a hole in the floor so it could be seamlessly
grafted onto the grotesque body that the make-up
department had created for her.

When Johner asks Ripley, "So I hear you, like, ran into
these things before. What did you do?", she replies, "I
died." Left on the cutting room floor was Johner's
remark, "That's not exactly what I was hoping to hear."

The script and promotional material reveal that the
orbit of Auriga was beyond Pluto. The project was not
approved by the Congress, possibly due to its hazardous
nature.

According to the script the USS military cultivated
vast quantities of cannabis to fund the cloning program
since they could not rely on the goverment for an
official subsidization. The goverment could not observe
the military beyond the boundaries of the solar system.

Although this subplot was dropped from the film there
are still hints of this backstory when Elgyn remarks
that the operation was not authorized by the Congress

and that Auriga is located in unregulated space. This also explains the assertion of Call that Dr Wren is conducting illegal experiments.

The alien eggs were made to appear more vivid and pulsating at the request of director Jean-Pierre Jeunet.

After watching Alien (1979), he thought the eggs were too static.

The ricocheting bullet that takes out a soldier standing behind Gary Dourdan was an unused idea from Jean-Pierre Jeunet's The City of Lost Children (1995).

The Newborns' skull was made of plaster so that it could be sucked out of the window into space. Cast only at 1/8-1/4" thick, it was scored into various pieces. Each piece was individually attached to a wire, so that when struck against the window and cracked, each fragment could be pulled out one by one.

The film's model miniatures were shot at a former Howard Hughes aircraft plant in Los Angeles. Visual effects supervisor Erik Henry and visual effects director of photography Rick Fichter used an advanced motion control camera system that required constant vigilance and re-alignment as the area was prone to small earthquakes and tremors.

Elgyn's spoken landing code for the Auriga is, of course, "EA-TM-E".

The gaps between the four Alien films steadily decreased. There was seven years between the release of Alien (1979) and Aliens (1986), six between Aliens and Alien³ (1992), and five between Alien³ and Alien: Resurrection (1997).

Ripley's outfit was going to be a different one than the dark red uniform she is wearing for the most of the film. After Sigourney Weaver saw Kim Flowers (Hillard) on the set, she wanted to wear the same costume. Hillard can be seen in the exact same outfit in the underwater scene.

Paul W.S. Anderson was in talks to direct but was unable to take part due to scheduling conflicts. Anderson would still get his chance to direct an outer space opus the following year with Event Horizon (1997). And of course he would visit the Alien franchise several years later with AVP: Alien vs. Predator (2004).

The scene with Ripley waking up gradually was not in the script. It was an addition by the director in order to symbolize the creation of the clone as a larva which transforms into a butterfly and tears up the cocoon.

In Call's back-story: When the android industry declined. The second generation androids or Autons (androids designed by androids) were developed, after an attempt to revitalize the android industry. The Autons rebel and only a few androids escaped the massacre and Call was created as a Auton secret agent and joined the Betty crew as a mechanic, so she could destroy the cloned xenomorphs aboard the Auriga.

Writer Joss Whedon wrote Christie's character with Yun-Fat Chow in mind. Yun-Fat's manager and producer Terence Chang turned down the role for him.

During the production of the Alien Quadrilogy DVD set, Frantic Films was brought in to re-shoot the title sequence where the bug's teeth gives way to a shot of the Auriga.

Danny Boyle was Fox's first choice to direct. He turned it down to work on A Life Less Ordinary (1997).

For the luckless human victims which the renegades find, already having had the aliens burst out of their stomachs, the crew devised costumes which had stomach entrails stitched onto the outside. This was directly inspired by a T-shirt that was popular around the time of the release of Alien (1979) in which an alien fetus (and a lot of blood) was attached to the front.

Producer David Giler was initially opposed to the making of a fourth film.

The first draft of the script contained an action sequence that took place in a garden contained within the spaceship "Auriga," with Ripley driving an electrically-powered jeep to avoid aliens attacking from all sides. This was to take place after the scene in the chapel but before the sequence where the Newborn is introduced. The sequence was cut due largely to budget constraints.

Jean-Pierre Jeunet originally wanted to cast a woman as the main villain but the studio refused, seeing as the film already had two female leads.

When the two aliens kill the third to get out of their cell, the intestines and guts and blood 'melting' through the floor was actually a descending platform with the intestines over top of it.

Nigel Phelps based the design of the spaceship "Betty"
on a jackhammer. The "Auriga" was originally to be a
vertical structure, but he abandoned this idea once he
realized the difficulty of capturing the scope of such
a ship design on film.

The money General Perez passes to Elgyn early in the
film portrays the face of producer Bill Badalato. The
prop money was handed out to the cast and crew after
the film was finished shooting.

Jean-Pierre Jeunet's long time partner, Marc Caro, with
whom he had made Delicatessen (1991) and The City of
Lost Children (1995), had no interest in taking part in
the film. Caro did fly out to Los Angeles for several
weeks to provide some costume and art direction
designs.

The tube where the clone of Ripley is created was
scripted as a regular bed like case, much like the cryo
tubes in which the hosts of the aliens are carried by
the Betty crew. It was an artistic choice to render the
glass chamber vertical shaped.

The 2nd film which Ron Perlman has played a space
pirate. 13 years earlier, Perlman played the space
pirate Zeno in the 1984 science fiction comedy film
"The Ice Pirates".

Michael Wincott would also play another space pirate in
his career, namely in Treasure Planet (2002).

The name of the girl Ripley was trying to remember near
the end of the Special Edition of the movie is Rebecca
'Newt' Jorden, who appeared in Aliens (1986).

Jean-Pierre Jeunet's first solo credit as a director.

The Betty is a space freighter. Written as a nod to the
Nostromo space freighter in the original "Alien", which
Ripley made her first terrifying encounter with the
alien.

Leland Orser's character is called Larry Purvis in the
credits. In the original script, he was supposed to

have his last name on his jumpsuit, and Christie calls him by that name. This scene was changed in the final cut, and the only person who ever refers to him as Purvis is Call, when they get ready to put him in the Betty's freezing chamber towards the end of the film.

The final of four Alien movies starring Sigourney Weaver.

The characters of Ripley and Call and the relationship between the two characters were strongly influenced by Xena and Gabrielle, the main characters from the TV show "Xena: Warrior Princess".

The crew of The Betty are space pirates. Joss Whedon would later create a science fiction TV show about a crew of space pirates called "Firefly".

General Perez (Dan Hedaya) was initially scripted to die in a decompression scene, with him being sucked through a small hole in a window. However, Jean-Pierre Jeunet thought this was a much too spectacular death for such a minor character, so this idea was instead used for the death of the Newborn. Perez's eventual death scene (with him being bitten in the back of his head, and observing a piece of his own brain) was not approved by the studio, but kept in the movie after test audiences responded quite favorably.

In the scene where Ripley discovers all of the other "failed" alien/hybrid clones
of herself, she finds one still alive who begs Ripley to mercy-kill her, to which Ripley does so with a flame thrower. This idea was recycled from a deleted scene from Alien (1979), where in the cut scene from that movie, Ripley finds Dallas and he asks her to mercy-kill him, which she does so with a flamethrower in a similar manner.

To achieve the shot where the camera travels inside Leland Orser to see the alien fetus about to be birthed, Orser had a camera shoved down his throat and then pulled out. This was then reversed.

The Special Edition includes a scene which eliminates controversy about the extent of damages caused by the collision course of Auriga. Call re-calibrates the velocity and the coordinates of Auriga so that the space station will crash onto an uninhabited quadrant of Earth. Not only this is consistent with Call's intentions of saving mankind and not inflict any human casualties but this also ensures that after the impact the repercussions of the wave will not cause any harm.

The film ends with the Newborn being sucked out of a tiny hole in the spaceship's hull, an idea that was considered for the first film but abandoned because of budgetary constraints. It was also proposed for dispatching a minor character in one of the drafts of Alien³ (1992).

The final chestburster was not intended to die during the climactic gunfire. According to the script the leads would chase the chestburster inside the Betty not wanting to risk damaging the hull with bullets. Call would stab it with her stileto.

The film originally ended with the Betty landing on Earth and Ripley and Call viewing the ruins of Paris. The scene was shot but the idea was abandoned for the theatrical release. When Jean-Pierre Jeunet was invited to create a Special Edition of the movie, the idea was revived and the scene's visual effects finished.

The first draft of the script included a different
climactic fight between Ripley, Call, and the Newborn.
Originally, after the Betty crash-landed on Earth,
Ripley and Call were to battle the Newborn on a snowy
mountain, using a "Harvester", a reaper-like farm
machine which they had found during the garden chase
sequence (which was also cut from the film due to
budget limits).

AVP: Alien vs. Predator (2004)
101 min - Action | Adventure | Sci-Fi - 13 August
2004 (USA)

During an archaeological expedition on Bouvetøya Island
in Antarctica, a team of archaeologists and other
scientists find themselves caught up in a battle
between the two legends. Soon, the team realize that
only one species can win.

Director: Paul W.S. Anderson
Writers: Dan O'Bannon ("Alien" characters), Ronald
Shusett ("Alien" characters)
Stars: Sanaa Lathan, Lance Henriksen, Raoul Bova

-A Couple Of Average Joe's
Take two gory R-rated franchises, mix them with a lame
connection story involving pyramids in Antarctica, and
clean it up for a PG-13, family friendly, rating and
you get this disappointment. The characters are boring,
the dialogue is laughable, and the only thing to root
for is the end credits. There are some cool AVP kills
but, it all seems wasted. Even the directors cut is
pointless. Bad script writing and studio tampering are
more apparent than a chest bursting scene.

In an interview, director Paul W.S. Anderson said that
Arnold Schwarzenegger offered to reprise his role as
Dutch Schaeffer (from Predator (1987)) at the end of
this movie as a cameo, but only if he lost the election
for California governor.

Except for scenes with stand-ins, Ian Whyte played all
of the Predators. He was the first Predator actor since
Kevin Peter Hall who died in 1991.

The Antarctic setting on Bouvet Island is based on the
unexplained "Vela Incident" of September 22, 1979,
where a satellite recorded a flash of light near the
island. It was first speculated to have been a man made
nuclear explosion or a natural event such as a meteor
strike, but this has never been resolved.

The heroine calling an Alien an "ugly mother..." is a
reference to the two previous Predator films, in which

both Arnold Schwarzenegger (Predator (1987)) and Danny Glover (Predator 2 (1990)) refer to the Predators as such.

When Lex asks Sebastian how to say "scared shitless" in Italian, he replies "Non vedo l'ora di uscire da questa piramide con te, perché mi sto cagando addosso." Translated, this literally means "I can't wait to get out of this pyramid with you, because I'm shitting myself."

Paul W.S. Anderson rewarded hardcore Alien and Predator fans by scattering references to the individual franchises within his film. For instance, the opening shot of the movie appears to be a silhouette of the Alien Queen from Aliens (1986), before being completely revealed as a Weyland Satellite.

Was rumored to be in development ever since a skull from the title characters in the Alien film series appeared in the spaceship trophy room in Predator 2 (1990).

The character of Verheiden was named after comic book writer Mark Verheiden, creator of the first Alien vs Predator comic series and the first story involving both species. Contrary to popular belief, the comic was released prior to the infamous shot of the alien "skull" in Predator 2 (1990).

While this film languished in so-called "development hell" for years, 20th-Century Fox considered producing a fifth film in the "Alien" franchise instead. James Cameron, who wrote and directed Aliens (1986), had written a script and even approached Sigourney Weaver to star and Ridley Scott to direct, both of whom expressed interest. When the studio decided to use the Alien/Predator crossover story instead, Cameron, Weaver and Scott all distanced themselves from the project, and later, declared they would never work on either franchise again. Several years later, Ridley Scott ended up reworking his pitch into his Alien prequel Prometheus (2012).

This is the first Alien film, and also the first Predator film, to get a rating other than R.

The first film in the "Alien" franchise to not feature Sigourney Weaver, who has said in interviews the idea of the crossover "sounded awful".

The words "alien" and "predator" are never said in this movie. Aliens are called "things", "creatures", and "serpents". Predators are referred to as "hunters" and "humanoids".

The green glow stick dropped down the shaft contains the same fluorescent liquid used by the effects departments of all the Predator movies as the Predators' blood. According to Predator (1987) director John McTiernan, they stumbled on the effect after unconvincing attempts to make the blood look orange forced the crew to look for alternatives.

Peter Weller was at one stage attached to appear in a cameo as John Yutani, the other half of the infamous "Weyland-Yutani" Company from the "Alien" films.

The character played by Lance Henriksen, Charles Bishop Weyland, is a co-founder of the Weyland Yutani Corporation. This is "the company" referred to in the earlier "Alien" movies. He is the "ancestor" of the Bishop Android from Aliens (1986) and Alien^3 (1992), who were also played by Henriksen. In his office on the ship, he does the same hand trick as the Android in "Aliens."

In the official theatrical trailer, there is a brief shot of the prison planet Fury 161 from Alien³ (1992).

At the beginning of the film, the readout of the Predator ship is shown reflected in the visor of the predator mask, just as in Alien (1979) the readouts of the Nostromo were reflected on the space helmets.

According to director Paul W.S. Anderson, if they'd filmed in Hollywood, the sets would have cost them $20 million. In Prague, they only cost $2 million, an important factor in keeping the film's budget down below $50 million.

The altars where victims were placed in the Chamber of Sacrifices of the pyramid is arranged identically to the hibernation pods in the original Alien (1979) movie.

The morse code picked up by the satellite at the beginning of the film spells out the words, "Whoever wins, we lose". This is, of course, the tagline used to promote the film.

The shot taken from inside the pyramid of the team approaching the top with their flashlights references the shot in Alien (1979) of the Nostromo's expedition team walking up to the entrance of the derelict.

Guillermo del Toro was offered the director's chair but opted to make Hellboy (2004) instead.

The most commercially successful of both Alien and Predator movies, grossing over $172 million.

Several hundred actresses tested for the lead female. Sanaa Lathan was selected one week before filming began, and had to fly to Prague immediately.

The Alien vs. Predator story crossed over virtually all forms of media before becoming a feature film. There was a successful comic book series, toy line, multiple video games, soundtrack (of the PC game) and even a trading card series.

At one stage both Peter Weller and Gary Busey were approached to do a cameo as John Yutani, the other founder of the infamous "Weyland-Yutani" Company from the "Alien" films, but Yutani was written out of the script. The character was later used in the sequel, Aliens vs. Predator: Requiem (2007), this time as a female.

The animatronic Queen was controlled by a motion-control rig which could save her movements digitally. So, if the Queen made a nice looking move in rehearsal, the move could be replayed verbatim in front of the camera.

The scene in which Weyland's team discovers the sacrificial chamber inside the pyramid was originally longer than seen in the theatrical cut. After Rousseau and Thomas discuss the hole in the corpse's chest, Sebastian finds a calcified facehugger. Lex and Sebastian then theorize as to what the creature's origin could be.

The design in the center of the floor of the sacrificial chamber is almost identical to the artwork of the Alien³ (1992) poster.

Lance Henriksen was first to be cast to maintain some kind of continuity with the previous films.

Paul W.S. Anderson stepped down from directing Resident Evil: Apocalypse (2004) (although he did stay on as producer) and directing Mortal Kombat to write and direct this film.

This film had both the shortest filming and post-production schedules of any "major studio" film in 2004; filming was given 2 1/2 months, while post-production was given just 4 months to complete.

After the opening credits are shown, SFX designers Tom Woodruff Jr. and Alec Gillis have brief cameos as technicians who discover the heat bloom coming from the pyramid.

Around the time of the film's release, it was reported that at a special industry screening, director Paul W.S. Anderson had said that the film was always planned as an R-rated movie and shot that way, but only three weeks prior to release the studio changed that by severely cutting the film for a lower PG-13 rating. This account has been heavily disputed by original "AvP" writer Peter Briggs. It was later revealed that this "press-screening" never actually took place, and was only an Internet rumor started
by fans. Anderson has said in interviews that the film seen in theaters is the version he intended audiences to see.

AVP was not screened for critics.

When one of the explorers is searching the whaling
compound and walks past a door to a building, there is
a shot from within the building in which the red light
from the guy's flare comes through the crack in the
door to form a flat vertical beam that's picked up by
the dust/snow from inside the room, just like the blue-
green scanner from the salvage scene at the beginning
of Aliens (1986).

The role of Max Stafford was written specifically for
Colin Salmon.

At Amalgamated Dynamics Incorporated, the workshop crew
nicknamed the 3 Predator characters Scar (main
Predator), Celtic, and Chopper.

Screenwriter Peter Briggs wrote his original spec
script for "Alien vs Predator" in 1991. The script sold
overnight and made him the subject of numerous magazine
and book "success story" articles. His version went
adrift following studio politics in the wake of
executive Joe Roth's departure from 20th Century Fox.

At the beginning of the film, the technician in the
satellite control station has a "drinking" bird among
the Tweety Pie dolls. These are the same birds that
were seen on the dining room table in Alien (1979) and
the abandoned prison canteen at the end of Alien[3]
(1992).

20th Century Fox wanted Roland Emmerich to direct the
film back in the late 1990's, due to the box office
success of Independence Day (1996), but Emmerich turned
down the offer, choosing to work on other projects.

First Predator movie to feature a left-handed predator.

This was a project that had floated around for about 10
years. It was only when director Paul W.S. Anderson did
his verbal pitch to the suits at 20th Century Fox that
anyone showed any real interest. So much so, in fact,
that they greenlit the film immediately.

There's a shot where the heroine pulls herself up a
cliff. It's filmed exactly like the shot in Alien
(1979) where Ripley (Sigourney Weaver) does the same,

looking for the Alien, and in Aliens (1986), when Ripley pulls herself out of the airlock at the end. In both shots the characters are sweating heavily and one of their hands in front of their faces can be seen.

On the official poster for the movie, with the Predator in the lower right corner and the alien in the upper right, drooling; the raised black parts of the alien's jaw, along with the opening in its mouth, spell out the letters AVP in an organic version of the font used for the movie's title.

The theatrical trailer includes soundbite samples from the original trailer for Alien (1979) and Bret (Harry Dean Stanton) screaming.

Brett Leonard, Chuck Russell, Joe Johnston and Robert Cohen were all considered for directing the movie at one point.

Screenwriter Shane Salerno was the last writer and "closer" on AVP: Alien vs. Predator (2004). He worked on the film for 15 months, including prior to production, through filming in Prague and all the way through post production without receiving the co-screenplay by credit that 20th Century Fox recommended him for to the WGA. Shane has a co-screenplay credit on the novelization of the film, dozens of magazine articles, and many of the original theatre posters.

The drawings that Paul W.S. Anderson used for his original presentation to 20th Century Fox were done by Patrick Tatopoulos.

Although the original cut runs 100 minutes, 12 of those minutes are credits.

At one point, David Twohy was once approached by Fox Studios back in May 2000 about his availability to write and direct the film, but turned down the offer due to scheduling conflicts.

With the filming of this movie Lance Henriksen became the second actor to be attacked and/or killed by an Alien, A Predator and The Terminator. Bill Paxton was the first.

Body Count: 65. (including Xenomorphs & Predators)

Previous movies in the "Alien" franchise (particularly Alien^3 (1992)) have established that the Alien creatures take on some physical characteristics of the creatures they gestate inside. This film ends with an alien "chestburster" emerging from inside a Predator; the creature has green coloration, an obvious resemblance to the Predator face, and makes the trademark "clicking" noise.

Alien Vs. Predator 2

Aliens vs. Predator: Requiem (2007)
"AVPR: Aliens vs Predator - Requiem" (original title)
 94 min - Action | Horror | Sci-Fi - 25 December
2007 (USA)

Warring alien and predator races descend on a small
town, where unsuspecting residents must band together
for any chance of survival.

Directors: Colin Strause (as The Brothers Strause) ,
Greg Strause (as The Brothers Strause)
Writers: Shane Salerno, Dan O'Bannon ("Alien"
characters),
Stars: Reiko Aylesworth, Steven Pasquale, John Ortiz

-A Couple Of Average Joe's
Since things didn't work out in Antarctica, let's try a
small town in Colorado this time. This film comes off
as a rip off of The Crazies but with aliens and some
video game elements thrown in. Last time we checked,
the alien xenomorphs were simple killers with a
particular life cycle. This time, they seem to have
more abilities than there are gadgets in a Bond film.
The atomic ending helps to eras all evidence of an
alien invasion. Too bad this film wasn't destroyed with
it. Better than AVP but that's not saying much.

Bill Paxton was approached to play the diner chef so he
could appear in the second 'Predator', 'Alien' and
'AvP' film in each series. However, scheduling
conflicts prevented him from making an appearance.

It was at one time hoped to include scenes of the
Aliens' home world. Conceptual art was created and it
was even storyboarded to be used as the closing shot of
the movie, but ultimately the idea was dropped in favor
of using it in a potential third film.

At the cemetery sequence, the man with a gun stands in
front of a tombstone with the name "HAWKINS" on it.
Hawkins was one of the soldiers with Dutch (Arnold
Schwarzenegger) on the first Predator (1987) movie,
played by Shane Black, today a screenwriter (Lethal

Weapon franchise) and director (Kiss Kiss Bang Bang (2005)).

In the original script, the Pred-Alien was to have died when the Predator ship crashed which occurred on page 3 or 4 of the script. It was re-written to incorporate the creature into the movie and make it the main villain as the studio was very impressed by the concept.

Danny Glover, who starred in Predator 2 (1990) was considered to reprise his role as Mike Harrigan but as a retired cop.

It was decided at an early stage that this movie would be R-rated as "it is what the fans want from the series".

This is the first movie in both the Predator and the AVP-based movies that actually feature scenes of the Predators' home planet.

According to the DVD commentary, Robert Joy's character Col. Stevens was originally written as Garber from Predator 2 (1990), who was the highest ranking survivor from Peter Keyes team hunting the predators. When the actor who played Garber (Adam Baldwin) couldn't be scheduled, the character was changed to Col Stevens.

This marks the second movie Ian Whyte has played the Predator creature. Next to Kevin Peter Hall, he is the only other actor to do so.

The Predator was nicknamed "Wolf" by the filmmakers, after the character Winston Wolfe in Pulp Fiction (1994). His role in the film, like Wolfe's, is described as that of a "cleaner" - one who covers up assassinations, accidents, and other messy situations.

Sound effects from previous films in both franchises were used in this film.

The Predalien was nicknamed "Chet" on set and in the script. This was to avoid early spoilers about the nature of the creature (i.e. it being a hybrid between the Alien and Predator). The name "Chet" was a reference to the obnoxious brother from the movie Weird Science (1985) (who was played by Bill Paxton).

Not screened for critics.

Colin Strause and Greg Strause both wanted the film to be 3-D, however the idea was dropped, because it would be too expensive.

This is special effects maestro Tom Woodruff's fourth time in the alien costume.

A voice artist was brought in to perform various Predator noises after the directors realized that audio samples and tapes containing the original sound effects had been either destroyed or of poor quality.

The eight-wheeled armored fighting vehicle is an M1126 Stryker derived from the Canadian LAV III and produced by General Dynamics Land Systems, in use by the United States Army. The vehicle is named for two American servicemen who posthumously received the Medal of Honor: Pfc Stuart S. Stryker, who died in World War II and Spc4 Robert F. Stryker, who died in the Vietnam War.

Antti Jokinen was offered a chance to direct.

This is the first time in the franchise that a Chestburster emerges from a child.

The bomb used to blow up the town at the end of the movie is shown to have a blast yield of 200 kilotons (about 10 times more powerful than the one used on Nagasaki).

According to the DVD commentary, effects artists Alec Gillis and Tom Woodruff Jr. mention that they originally had an effects sequence that would've shown us the Predator actually skinning the body of Deputy Ray Adams. But the idea was dropped when Fox Studios that is was deemed "too horrific".

The Yutani character (of the "Weyland-Yutani" Company from the "Alien" films) was originally going to appear in the AVP: Alien vs. Predator (2004), but was written out. The character was originally conceived to be male.

Several sounds are intentionally recycled from previous 'Alien' and 'Predator' movies as tribute to those films. These include (but are not limited to): actual Predator (like growls and tracking sounds from the helmet) and Alien noises (like hissing and screeching); the beeping of the motion tracker from Aliens (1986), used in this movie during the opening credits, and as the sound made on the tracking screen showing the bomber heading towards its target; and the computers around Col. Stevens make the same sounds as the Mother computer from Alien (1979). The only original sound that could not be reused was the Predator's characteristic chirruping sound, which was recreated specifically for this movie.

Steven Pasquale's character "Dallas Howard" shares his name with Tom Skerritt's character from the original Alien (1979) movie - Dallas was the captain of the Nostromo. Moreover, he says the line "Get to the chopper!", which was also said by Dutch (Arnold Schwarzenegger) in Predator (1987). Perhaps a coincidence, he also shares his name with actress Bryce Dallas Howard who does not appear in any of these series.

Prometheus
Prometheus (I) (2012)
 124 min - Adventure | Mystery | Sci-Fi - 8 June
2012 (USA)

Following clues to the origin of mankind a team journey
across the universe and find a structure on a distant
planet containing a monolithic statue of a humanoid
head and stone cylinders of alien blood but they soon
find they are not alone.

Director: Ridley Scott
Writers: Jon Spaihts, Damon Lindelof
Stars: Noomi Rapace, Logan Marshall-Green, Michael
Fassbender

-A Couple Of Average Joe's
Ridley Scott's attempt at making a prequel to his Alien
film is a mixed bag of beautiful set designs and
effects, with a story that screams of studio tampering.
Most of the characters are boring and Noomi Rapace as
the films lead is no Ripley. Michael Fassbender as an
android is fascinating, Idris Elba is underused and
Charlize Theron is bland and lifeless (android?). When
everything is said and done, it all comes off as a big
tease. An unintentionally hilarious moment comes from
the makeup worn by Guy Pearce to make him appear as

elderly. Instead he looks like a young "guy" in a
costumer pretending to be an old man.

Ridley Scott decided against featuring Xenomorphs (the
titular Alien of the film series) in the film, as "the
sequels squeezed him dry, he did very well... and no
way am I going back there." Instead, this being an
indirect prequel to Alien (1979), he decided to feature
a Xenomorph ancestor/parent.
- This has since been disputed by Ridley Scott, saying
he wanted to make a direct sequel to Alien/Aliens and
depict the home world of the "Engineers" but the studio
didn't want this project to be linked to the Alien
franchise.

During production, Ridley Scott kept the use of
computer-generated imagery as low as possible, using
CGI mainly in space scenes; Scott recalled advice
VFXpert Douglas Trumbull gave him on the set of Blade

Runner (1982): "If you can do it live, do it live", and also claimed that practical VFX was more cost-effective than digital VFX.

Director Ridley Scott named the film "Prometheus", seeing the name aptly fit the film's themes: "It's the story of creation; the gods and the man who stood against them." In Greek mythology, the Titan Prometheus was a servant of the gods, who stole and gave to mankind the gift of fire, an immeasurable benefit that changed the human race forever (for better AND worse).

Designer H.R. Giger, who worked on the original design of the Xenomorph Alien (1979), was brought in to assist in reverse-engineering the design of the Aliens in the film.

To prepare for his role as the android David, Michael Fassbender watched Blade Runner (1982) (a Ridley Scott film), The Man Who Fell to Earth (1976), The Servant (1963) and Lawrence of Arabia (1962) (mentioned by Peter Weyland). Fassbender also studied Olympic diver Greg Louganis, drawing inspiration from Louganis's physicality.

The "beginning of time" sequence that opens the film was shot in Iceland. The whole shoot took two weeks to complete.

Composer Marc Streitenfeld had the orchestra play his compositions backwards, and then digitally reversed the compositions for the final film. This made the music sound unusual and unsettling, which he felt was right for the film.

Charlize Theron found herself struggling during her action scenes due to her smoking habit, particularly the segments that required her to run through sand in boots weighing 30 pounds (14 kg).

Charlize Theron was originally cast as Elizabeth Shaw, but had to decline the role due to scheduling conflicts. Later, another change in schedule freed Theron to do the film, thus allowing her to take the role of Meredith Vickers, as Noomi Rapace had already taken the role of Shaw.

In one of the screenplay drafts for Alien (1979), there was a sex scene between Ripley and Dallas, to show how crew members would engage in casual sex during long space travels, simply to fulfill their needs. Ridley Scott never filmed the scene, but the idea was reused for this film in the exchange between Vickers and Janek.

Ridley Scott instructed Charlize Theron to stand in corners and move in lurking movements, in order to accentuate Vickers's distant, enigmatic nature.

While Ridley Scott suggested that the cast could have slept and effectively "lived" on the Prometheus interior set during initial filming, this didn't happen due to health and safety precautions.

Ridley Scott suggested that an Engineer was sent to Earth to stop humanity's increasing aggression, but was crucified; the implication being that it was Jesus Christ. He felt though that this would be too obvious a religious allegory for the film.

According to Ridley Scott, the film's plot was inspired by Erich von Däniken's writings about ancient astronauts: "Both NASA and the Vatican agree that it is almost mathematically impossible that we can be where we are today, without there being a little help along the way. That's what we're looking at: we are talking about gods and engineers, engineers of space. Were the Aliens designed as a form of biological warfare, or biology that would go in and clean up a planet?"

During the scene in which the Hammerpede erupts from Millburn's corpse, Ridley Scott did not inform Kate Dickie about what was to occur in the scene and thus her screaming reaction was real.

Ridley Scott stated that he was filming "the most aggressive film [he] could" by not caring about MPAA ratings, having support for such bold movement from 20th Century Fox CEO Tom Rothman, who addressed Alien (1979) fans by saying that he was "very aware of their concern", and that "they can take it that the film will not be compromised either way. So if that means that the film is R, then it'll be an R. If it's PG-13, then it'll be a PG-13, but it will not be compromised." Scott shot the film with both adult-only R and more accessible PG-13 film ratings in mind, allowing the more adult content to be cut if necessary without harming the overall presentation, given the case it was asked to be cut down. Eventually, the film was rated "R for Sci-Fi violence including some intense images, and brief language", and it was released without any demanded cuts.

The Swedish actress Noomi Rapace, who plays British character Shaw, worked on set with a dialect coach to help her achieve the closest accent she could manage.

In 2002, Aliens (1986) director James Cameron discussed ideas for a fifth Alien (1979) film with Ridley Scott, with the intention that Cameron would produce the film with Scott directing, and Sigourney Weaver returning to star in the lead role of Ripley. However upon discovering that 20th Century Fox were developing the crossover film AVP: Alien vs. Predator (2004), Cameron ceased all work on the project, believing that the crossover would "kill the validity of the franchise". Though Cameron went on to state that he would never again work with the Alien franchise, Scott eventually ended up reworking their idea into this film.

An innovative viral campaign was used to promote the film, consisting of several videos depicting the near future world from the film. The first was a fake TED Talk given by Peter Weyland (played by Guy Pearce), dated 2023. Later, two different versions of a commercial promoting the David 8 android (played by Michael Fassbender) were released. These viral videos were designed by Ridley Scott and Damon Lindelof themselves, and were directed by Scott's son, Luke Scott.

When Prometheus approaches the landing zone, straight marks on the ground can be seen which are very similar to the Nazca lines located in the Nazca Desert in southern Peru. The Nazca lines are considered by few rogue scientists/archaeologists to be runways of an ancient airfield used by extraterrestrials. This idea was popularized by Swiss author, Erich von Däniken, and is generally regarded as pseudo-science. One of the more prevailing and accepted theories posits that the lines were part of the religious practices of the local people. Other theories place astronomical, cosmological or topographical significance to them.

As mentioned in the film, the original Prometheus was a character from Greek mythology. He was a Titan (an immortal older god), who gave the gift of fire to human beings. Prometheus was punished for this by being bound to a rock in Hades (the Greek underworld), where each day an eagle, the emblem of Zeus, was sent to feed on his liver, only to have it grow back to be eaten again the next day. In some stories, Prometheus is freed at last by the hero Heracles (Hercules). Among the ancient Greeks, Prometheus was venerated as a deity. Prometheus may derive from the Greek for "forethinker", or the Proto-Indo-European for "thief", Prometheus also tricked the gods, which is of relevance to this film.

The three-triangle logo of the Weyland corporation (while visually similar to that of the actual Weinstein Group) is actually derived from a pattern appearing on the wall in the background of an early Ron Cobb production painting of the "Space Jockey" for the original Alien (1979) film. The logo can be seen as part of David's fingerprint.

Ridley Scott described the Engineers as "tall, elegant dark angels." Concept designers Neville Page and Carlos Huante cite Greco-Roman gods, the works of J.W. Turner (a painter whose trademark was brightness) and William Blake (a painter who employed religious symbolism), the Statue of Liberty, Michaelangelo's David, and Elvis Presley as visual influences for the design of the Engineer.

According to Ridley Scott, the spherical helmets were inspired by a Steve Jobs story where he built an office entirely out of industrial-strength glass: "If I'm in 2083 and I'm going into space, I want something where I have 360 vision. By then, glass will be light and you won't be able to break it with a bullet."

Ann Scibelli created the sound of glistening ice forming on the stone cylinders by applying Pop Rocks (carbonated candy) to materials like wet metal and stone and then spraying the materials with water to produce the "popping, cracking" sound.

Sound designer Ann Scibelli's recorded sounds of her pet parrot over several weeks. Her vocalizations which were then used in the film as beeps, alarms and the cries of Shaw's alien offspring.

During the on location segment shoot in Iceland (the movie's opening sequence), Noomi Rapace, who was partly raised there, was able to visit her family.

Noomi Rapace landed the role of Elizabeth when a scheduled meeting in Los Angeles with producer Michael Costigan instead led to an unexpected meeting with Ridley Scott. When Scott announced that he'd seen The Girl with the Dragon Tattoo (2009) three times and was very keen to work with her, Noomi accepted the offer right away.

This is not Ian Whyte's (who plays the Last Engineer) only attachment to the Alien (1979) films. Whyte also played the Predators in AVP: Alien vs. Predator (2004) and Aliens vs. Predator: Requiem (2007).

The first shot of the cave paintings at the beginning of the film, which showed a horse in motion, originate from the Chauvet Cave in the South of France, which was the subject of the Werner Herzog documentary Cave of Forgotten Dreams (2010), also shot in 3D.

When Janek talks with Vickers, he mentions that his accordion was property of Stephen Stills. Stills is a singer, former member of Buffalo Springfield and 'Crosby, Stills & Nash' and composer of "Love the One You're With", that Janek sings often times.

Was originally conceived as a prequel to Ridley Scott's Alien (1979), but Scott announced his decision to turn it into an original film with Noomi Rapace (who was already set to star) still in the cast as one of five main characters. Some time later it was confirmed that while the movie would take place in the same universe as Alien and greatly reference that movie, it would mostly be an original movie and not a direct prequel.

The Orrery was one of the most complex visual effects, containing 80-100 million polygons and taking several weeks to render as a single, complete shot.

Costume designer Janty Yates gave the characters unique
clothes that would represent their nature:
Vickers is dressed in an ice-silver silk mohair suit,
which signifies her icy nature David's outfit was given
finer lines to produce a more linear appearance and
emphasize his robotic nature Holloway is dressed in
hoods, fisherman pants, and flip-flops to look casual
and relaxed and Janek wears a canvas-greased jacket to
represent his long career at the helm of a ship.

Producers Walter Hill and David Giler rejoin Ridley
Scott for the first time in over 30 years since they
first collaborated on Alien (1979).

Ridley Scott approached SOAS, University of London, in
2011 to find experts who could help create a new
language for the film. Anil Biltoo from SOAS' Language
Centre worked to create the language, as well as the
alien script, which can be seen throughout. Anil Biltoo
can be seen briefly in a scene with Michael Fassbender.
Other SOAS staff members appear briefly and are
credited, including Wambui Kunya, Sonam Dugdak, Shin-
Ichiro Okajima, Kay Rienjang, Zed Sevcikova and Reynir
Thor Eggertsson.

The Hammerpede's design was inspired by translucent sea
creatures with visible arteries/veins/organs and
cobras.

To find a method of depicting the Engineer's DNA destruction, the VFXperts carved vein-like structures from silicone and pumped black ink/oils into them, and then filmed the changes occurring over an extended period of time.

Ridley Scott initially wanted Max von Sydow for the role of Peter Weyland. However, Scott and Damon Lindelof conceived of a scene in which David the android (Michael Fassbender) would interface with Weyland while in hypersleep, and that Weyland's dream would reflect his looks as a younger man since he is obsessed with immortality. Though the scene was cut from the script and never filmed, Guy Pearce had already been cast in the role and thus underwent extensive make-up to appear elderly.

When Shaw is discussing her finds around the world in the conference, the words "Eilean a' Cheo" can be seen in the background. This means "The Island of Mist" in Scottish Gaelic, and is a nickname for the Isle of Skye, properly called "An t-Eilean Sgitheanach".

Early drafts of the script had a scene on a colony on Mars where Peter Weyland (Guy Pearce) had his office. Though concept art was completed, the scene was removed for pacing reasons and never filmed.

Fifield's bright red mohawk hairstyle was designed by Sean Harris and Ridley Scott, based on Scott's sketch of a man with a "severe haircut"

For the scene of the Prometheus' descent to the alien moon LV-223, VFX art director Steven Messing referenced NASA imagery and aerial photographs of locations in Iceland and Wadi Rum. Messing painted over these images and combined them with 3D set extensions to create a realistic altered landscape.

The hologram star map scene was inspired by a painting "A Philosopher Lecturing on the Orrery."

Marks Ridley Scott's first venture in 3D feature filmmaking and his third sci-fi movie after Alien (1979) and Blade Runner (1982).

Gemma Arterton, Carey Mulligan, Olivia Wilde, Anne Hathaway, Abbie Cornish and Natalie Portman were considered for the role of Elizabeth Shaw.

The Vatican's official newspaper L'osservatore Romano gave a negative review of this film saying that it "mishandles the delicate questions raised by... the battle eternal between good and evil."

Orion's constellation can be seen in the holographic star chart during the explanation of Shaw and Holloway about Engineers. It appears to the left of Shaw.

Noomi Rapace wasn't yet born when Alien (1979) was first released.

Cinematographer Dariusz Wolski convinced Ridley Scott that it would be possible to shoot the film in 3D with the same ease and efficiency of typical filming. 3D company 3ality Technica provided some of the rigs and equipment to facilitate 3D filming, and trained the film's crew in their proper operation. Since 3D films need high lighting levels on set, the traditional dark shadowy atmosphere of the Alien films was added in post-production through grading processes, while the 3D equipment was based on post-Avatar (2009) technology.

Logan Marshall-Green described his role of Charlie Holloway as "an ESPN X-Games (1994) scientist" who leaps before he looks.

Michelle Yeoh and Angelina Jolie were originally considered for the role of Meredith Vickers.

The film was originally to be called "Paradise" (December 2010).

Patrick Wilson, playing Elizabeth Shaw's father, is only 6 years older than Noomi Rapace.

The first film to feature two actors who played Charlotte Brontë's creation of Edward Rochester in two different literary adaptations involving the same character in the same cast. Rafe Spall played Edward Rochester in Wide Sargasso Sea (2006) and Michael Fassbender played the same role in Jane Eyre (2011).

James Franco was considered for the role of Holloway.

There is a scene where characters discuss whether or not they should bring weapons to a scientific expedition. The same happened in AVP: Alien vs. Predator (2004), which similarly focused on scientists discovering that extraterrestrial life visited ancient Earth.

In the scene where Peter Weyland is being awoken from hibernation, a prop in the background is actually an ACL TOP coagulation analyzer.

Elizabeth shaw is also the name of the 3rd doctors scientific assistant in doctor who

Quite a few of the actors in this movie have also appeared in movies based on comic books. Michael Fassbender appears in the X-Men franchise, Charlize Theron was in Hancock and Aeon Flux, Idris Elba has been in Thor, Thor: The Dark World and Ghost Rider: Spirit of Vengence, Guy Pearce was in Iron Man 3, Patrick Wilson was in Watchmen, and Benedict Wong was in Kick-Ass 2.

In the sequence where a holographic Peter Weyland addresses the crew of the Prometheus, the musical underscore heard quotes the original theme to Alien written by Jerry Goldsmith but never used in the 1979 film.

Numerous white Stelton vacuum jugs appear in various interior shots of the Prometheus ship, including the ship's lab and Shaw's bedroom.

Ben Foster was rumored for a role.

The film contains approximately 1300 digital VFX shots.

Charlie Holloway says the same line, in the same manner as Cpl. Dwayne Hicks in Aliens. Prometheus: "David, We are leaving!" In Aliens: "Marines, we are leaving!"

This is the second movie Michael Fassbender worked on that had a main character named Shaw, the other was x-men first class.

When Elizabeth Shaw is having a C-Section to remove the alien from her body, the alien was wrapped in a condom filled with fake blood so that when it was pulled from her body, the condom could be punctured and explode violently.

When Prometheus approaches the alien solar system, it's mentioned that it's 3.27×10^{14} (327,000,000,000,000) km from Earth. That's 34.6 light years or 10.4 parsecs.

Shaw's final message at the end of the film closely mirrors that of Ripley's final log entry at the end of Alien (1979). Both messages include indication of being a "final log entry", description of the fates of the ships' respective crews, and identifying themselves as the "last surviving crew member of the (Nostromo/Prometheus)".

The moon's name in the film (LV223) is arguably a reference to the the bible verse Leviticus 22:3 - "Say to them, 'If any man among all your descendants throughout your generations approaches the holy gifts which the sons of Israel dedicate to the LORD, while he has an uncleanness, that person shall be cut off from before Me; I am the LORD.'" (New American Standard Bible). This foreshadows the events of the film, including the fates of the crew.

In May 7th, 2012, Guillermo del Toro declared that his long proposed adaptation for "At the Mountains of Madness" was indefinitely delayed as he felt Ridley Scott's film was extremely similar to the approach he penned for H.P. Lovecraft's novella, even to the point of having "scenes that would be almost identical. Both movies seem to share identical set pieces and the exact same big revelation (twist) at the end."

David idolizes British World War I hero T.E. Lawrence. In World War I, the British Army, including Lawrence, used a machine gun called the Vickers. Also, Peter Weyland, who quotes Lawrence of Arabia (1962), is the creator/synthetic father of David, but also the biological father of Meredith Vickers.

Ridley Scott originally said the movie would be released in late 2011, possibly 2012. In December 2010, it was rumoured that the prequels had been pushed back to 2013 and 2014. This was untrue and was apparently a failed attempt to cast Leonardo DiCaprio in the film who would have been busy filming another movie. The film is to be released June 8, 2012 in the US. It's released a week or so earlier in various other countries.

It was originally announced that Carl Rinsch would be directing the prequel with Ridley Scott producing it.

Things stalled for a while and Fox weren't keen on doing the movie unless Ridley Scott was the director. In July 2009, it was confirmed that Ridley Scott would be directing the prequel.

There was quite a few rumours for the female lead. Gemma Arterton, Carey Mulligan, Abbie Cornish, Natalie Portman and Olivia Wilde. Anne Hathaway and James Franco were also rumoured for parts. Apparently, Fox wanted Leonardo DiCaprio too.

It was revealed in September 2010 that Ridley Scott wanted an 18-certificate movie (Hard R Rating) and a $250M budget but Fox refused. In another report a few weeks later, Damon Lindelof had apparently finished the rewrites on Spaihts' script cutting large set pieces out and making the script PG13 friendly. In that report, it was stated that Ridley wanted a $150M budget.

Some title considerations were Alien: Origin, Alien: Genesis and Paradise.

Early drafts of the script had a scene on a colony on Mars where Peter Weyland (Guy Pearce) had his office. Though concept art was completed, the scene was removed for pacing reasons and never filmed.

According to Ridley Scott, the film's plot was inspired by Erich von Däniken's writings about ancient astronauts: "Both NASA and the Vatican agree that it is almost mathematically impossible that we can be where we are today, without there being a little help along the way. That's what we're looking at: we are talking about gods and engineers, engineers of space. Were the Aliens designed as a form of biological warfare, or biology that would go in and clean up a planet?"

Ridley Scott decided against featuring xenomorphs in the film, as "the sequels squeezed him dry, he did very well··· and no way am I going back there." Instead, this being an indirect prequel to Alien, he decided to feature a xenomorph ancestor/parent.

In 2002, Aliens director James Cameron discussed ideas for a fifth Alien film with Ridley Scott, with the intention that Cameron would produce the film with Scott directing, and Sigourney Weaver returning to star in the lead role of Ripley. However upon discovering that 20th Century Fox were developing the crossover film AVP: Alien vs. Predator, Cameron ceased all work on the project, believing that the crossover would "kill the validity of the franchise" . Though Cameron went on to state that he would never again work with the Alien franchise, Scott eventually ended up reworking their idea into this film.

Ridley Scott approached SOAS, University of London, in 2011 to find experts who could help create a new language for the film. Anil Biltoo from SOAS' Language Centre worked to create the language, as well as the alien script, which can be seen throughout. Anil Biltoo can be seen briefly in a scene with Michael Fassbender. Other SOAS staff members appear briefly and are credited, including Wambui Kunya, Sonam Dugdak, Shin-Ichiro Okajima, Kay Rienjang, Zed Sevcikova and Reynir Thor Eggertsson. Producers Walter Hill and David Giler rejoin Ridley Scott for the first time in over 30 years since they first collaborated on Alien.

H.R. Giger had a little involvement in production. Ridley Scott said he worked on the movie for 11 months just creating some murals for the first chamber the characters come across. On the Prometheus Blu-Ray, Giger was seen meeting with Ridley Scott and he did some sketches of the creatures. Scott said some of his ideas were interesting but he didn't enough time to pursue them. No mention of Giger creating the murals was mentioned in the Blu-Ray features.

The Thing (1982)
 109 min - Horror | Mystery | Sci-Fi - 25 June 1982
(USA)

Scientists in the Antarctic are confronted by a shape-
shifting alien that assumes the appearance of the
people that it kills.

Director: John Carpenter
Writers: Bill Lancaster (screenplay), John W. Campbell
Jr. (story)
Stars: Kurt Russell, Wilford Brimley, Keith David

-A Couple Of Average Joe's
Over thirty years later, this film looks great and it
still scares the hell out of you. Unless you speak
Norwegian, you won't know what the hell is going on at
the film's beginning. Each character has a distinctive
personality and actually makes you care about their
well being, unlike man of the two-dimensional
personalities we see in movies these days. Kurt Russell
is cool and sympathetic as McReady. The makeup effects
are brilliantly effective and the musical score is
disturbing in its simplicity. The tension is high and
it never lets up. BRAVO

The Thing as the first film in what Carpenter calls his
 "Apocalypse Trilogy," Prince of Darkness and Into the
Mouth of Madness.

The Thing film is based on John W. Campbell, Jr.'s
short story, Who Goes There?. A controversial editor
(Astounding Science Fiction) and writer (Twilight,
Night, The Incredible Planet), Campbell is credited
with having shaped modern science fiction.

Carpenter's film is more faithful to the novella.

The director wanted to begin the film with a flying
saucer in space, headed toward Earth and in homage to
The Thing from Another World

Russell's brother-in-law (at the time), Associate
Producer and first AD Larry Franco, is seen leaning out
of the helicopter.

Camera operator Ray Stella volunteered his arms for all the needle sticks— "He said he could do it all day

Before becoming an actor, Brimley worked as a wrangler and a ranch hand, a blacksmith, a bodyguard for Howard Hughes, and he began his acting career as a stunt man.

The dog Thing was created by Stan Winston (Iron Man, Aliens, Terminator 2: Judgement Day, Edward Scissorhands). The slime emitted from the Thing is carbopol, (according to Carpenter) "the stuff inside Twinkies.

The computer animation graphics were designed by Carpenter's college friend, John Wash—he also did graphics for Escape from New York.

Carpenter's wife at the time, Adrienne Barbeau ("Maude, Carnivàle," The Fog, Creepshow) did provide the computer voice.

One day after shooting a scene with the flamethrower, Russell pulled a practical joke on Carpenter by covering his face and head with bandages and claiming he had gotten burned.

The shot of MacReady walking to the small hole in the ice where the alien was buried was filmed on Universal's back lot. The surroundings were matte paintings.

Carpenter struggled with a way of making MacReady the Thing. He finally chose to leave the film ambiguous and just tease it.

One of the reviews for The Thing called Carpenter a "pornographer of violence".

50 people operated the Blair monster in The Thing.

Awesome random movie trivia at the end of the book.

Just when you thought it was over...

There is a potato and a shoe in the asteroid chase scene in Empire Strikes back.

The alien language in district 9 was created by rubbing a pumpkin.

Frank sinatra was offered the part of John Mcclane in Die Hard - to reprise his original role.

Cutthroat Island lost 147 million at the box office and contributed to Carolco's bankruptcy.

The great machine in contact was originally designed as a time machine in T2

At the end of Casablanca the airplane is a cutout.

The ground crew in casablanca at the end are little people.

The Breakfast Club was supposed to have a sequel every 10 years Nelson and Hughes hated each other.

The Bible andPplanet of the Apes are the only G-Rate movies to feature nudity.

Laurence Fishburne was 14 when he filmed his part in Apocalypse Now. he lied about his age.

Airplane! titles from around the world - Argentina "Where is the pilot?"

Airplane! titles from around the world - Brazil "Tighten Up Your Seatbelts The Pilots Are Gone!".

Airplane! titles from around the world - Spain - "Land As You Can".

Airplane! titles from around the world - Norway - "Help! We're Flying!".

Airplane! titles from around the world - France - "Is There A Pilot On This Plane?".

Airplane! titles from around the world - Germany "The Incredible Trip On A Crazy Plane".

A Nightmare On Elm St. was loosely based on a real event.

The word zombie is never used in Night Of The Living Dead.

The first U.S. movies released on VHS? Patton, Sound Of Music and MASH - 1977

The T-Rex wasn't supposed to break the glass in Jurassic Park - those are real screams of terror.

FBI Claimed that It's A Wonderful Life promoted communism.

JARVIS - Just Another Really Very Intelligent System - Iron Man.

JAFO - Just Another Fucking Observer - Blue Thunder.

Stoic From How To Train YOur Dragon would be 7'2 if he were real.

End Of Days was the last Dolby Digital movie released on Laserdisc.

Moanin Myrtle was 37 at the time she filmed the bath scene in the Harry Potter movies.

A real horsehead was used in The Godfather, John Marley freaked out.

Ghostbusters took place in the future as it was originally written.

Haley Joel Osmet was Forrest Gumps Son.

The Goblin King and Bruce from Finding Nemo - same guy.

Edward Norton's character's name is never mentioned in Fight Club.

Zorg and Korbin Dallas never met each other.

A proposed sequel to E.T. was going to be named Nocturnal Fears and E.T.'s name was Zreck.

Walk This Way by Aerosmith was influenced by Young Frankenstein when Marty Feldmen says "walk this way".

Spielbergs War Of The Worlds filming was inspired by amateur videos of 9/11.

The look of Axiom from Wall-E was inspired by Disneyland parks.

the original tag line for Twister? "It Sucks".

Orson Welle's final role was as Unicron in Transformers: The Movie

The first Toy Story contains no visible liquids, fiery explosions or long hair.

The fade to white at the end of total recall was Quaid getting lobotomized.

Paul Verhoeven revealed that Total Recall was actually a dream.

Dr. Edgemar outlines the entire 3rd act as he tries to tell Quaid nothing is real.

Keith David never removes his gloves during the thing - he broke his hand.

O.J. Simpson was up for the role of the Terminator, but nobody could see him in the role.

Marlon Brando was reading his lines from a diaper when he spoke to the baby Superman.

Tobey Maguire actually performed the stunt where he catches MJ's lunch.. after many takes.

Lord Farquaad from Shrek is based on Michael Eisner - supposedly.

Eisner used to call Katzenberg "evil Midget" hence Farquaad's shortness.

The Humane Society objected to the crow scene in Shawshank Redemption.

The crew had to find a maggot that died of natural causes before they could film the crow scene...

Brad Pitt threatened to quit Se7en if New Line changed the ending.

Spielberg refused pay for his work on Schindler's List.

In the TV version of Return of the Living Dead, Freddy's jacket says "tv version" instead of "fuck you".

Ezekiel monologue in Pulp Fiction was supposedly written for Keitels character in From Dusk 'Til Dawn.

Jim Caviezel was struck by lighting while filming the crucifixion scene in The Passion Of The Christ.

Many of the extras in One Flew Over The Cuckoo's nest were actual mental patients.

Cloud Atlas is the most expensive independent movie ever as of 2013.

Other Father in Coraline is singing of Other mothers true intentions.

Pinocchio can be seen in the Snuggly Ducklin in Tangled.

RIO was based on a true story.

Cabin In The Woods -Marty doesn't go swimming because he was in too good of shape.

Gene Hackman never shot a frame of footage for Superman II - it was reused footage from Superman with body doubles and voice impersonators.

McAvoy had to wear hair extensions for the first month of shooting X-Men First class - he had shaved his head prior to filming.

The Lost Boys was envisioned as a Goonies type film with 5th and 6th grade vampires.

The helicopter pilot at the beginning of Carpenter's The Thing spoils the entire plot, if you spoke Norwegian.

In the Alien series of films, the androids are named in alphabetical order Ash,Bishop Call and David.

Lion King Alternate ending - Scar defeats Simba by throwing him off pride rock, but is burned alive by wildfire.

The oxygen breathing fluid in the Abyss is real

Ewok was never uttered in any of the Star Wars movies.

The Estate of Dr Seuss said there will never be a live action movie after the disaster that was the Cat In The Hat.

Machete was in the first spy kids movie.

If you watch all of the Saw movies, you'll spend 666 minutes doing it.

Time travel movies are banned in China.

Godzilla's roar is copyrighted.

The Disney Cinderella castle is real - Neuschwanstein Castle, Germany

That blue light hovering above the egg chamber in Alien? It was a laser used by The Who, they were rehearsing next door.

George Lucas broke Bruce the shark when he visited the Jaws set and put his head in the mouth.

Showgirls was the most succesful widley released NC-17 movie. It still lost 25 million.

The Ten Commandments that you see on US Goverment property? Thank Cecli B. Demille. It was a publicity stunt.

christopher plummer was drunk during the music festival sequence of the Sound Of Music.

A sequel to Earthquake was written where the survivors now live in San Francisco and it happens again.

John Williams wrote the original score to the Poseidon adventure.

The studio insisted that quotes be put around "Crocodile" Dundee, so that the audience wouldn't be confused if Dundee was a crocodile.

How many balloons would it take to make a house fly? 12,658,392 helium filled balloons.

Dean Jones owns the only existing trick Herbie car from The Love Bug.

The first movie broadcast on television was The Crooked Circle in 1933.

Spoiler alert - none of the characters in Cabin Fever actually die from the disease.

Cameron Diaz is one of the subway passengers in Minority Report.

Watching the movie 2012 in North Korea is punishable by jail time. It's seen as an insult.

The sound of the alien spaceship's weapon exploding in Independence Day? it's James Brown screaming.

the urban legend of the ghost boy in Three Men and a Baby? It was created by the studio. The movie set home video records.

Bilbo's 111th birthday cake caught fire. Ian Holm finished the scene as it burned.

Steven Seagal was Sean Connery's martial arts trainer in Never Say Never Again. Seagal broke Connery's wrist.

White Castle was the only fast food chain that would allow the producers of Harold and Kumar to use their name.

the bulletproof cup scene in Super Troopers was filmed outside of a working prison to the cheers of the inmates.

The Legend of Ron Burgundy was inspired by Jessica Savitch's televised biograpy.

A sequel to 16 Candles was planned called 32 Candles. It would have taken place 16 years later.

16 candles sequel - USA network never wanted to have the original cast back. Thankfully it fell through.

The movie The Explorers was never finished. The studio released a work in progress cut.

Gremlins and Indian Jones and the Temple of Doom helped to influence the MPAA to create the PG-13 rating.

Slimer is the ghost of John Belushi.

Tron was disqualified from getting an Oscar. The Academy felt that using a computer was considered cheating.

Those are real pig entrails in the Captain Rhodes death scene from Dawn Of The Dead.

The pig entrailes used in Captain Rhodes death scene were stored in a fridge that was unplugged and they spoiled causing many on set to get sick.

Teen Wolf title in Brazil "Boy From The Future".

The santa that stabbed Simon Pegg in Hot Fuzz? Peter Jackson

Buttercup from The Princess Bride is technically not a princess.

David Bowies face is hidden several times in the background in Labyrinth.

Original title to Honey I shrunk the Kids? "Teenie Weenie".

Will Ferrell's balls in Step Brothers cost $20,000.

West Side Story was inspired by the short-lived phenomenon of real street gang dance fighting.

Triumph Of The Will was Hitler's attention-deficit attempt at making a sex tape - We kinda dispute this one, although it wouldn't surprise us.

SPECTRE stood for Special Executive for Counter-intelligence, Terrorism, Revenge and Extortion.

Nicholson pulled out a weapon on the set of The Departed to provoke a genuine reaction - he felt he wasn't intimidating enough during the Billy and Frank scene.

Jennifer Lawrence kicked Josh Hutcherson in the head during the Hunger Games, Hutcherson received a concussion from it.

One of the Bond girls used to be a man, baby.

The spider used in the 2002 Spiderman movie was a Steatoda spider..

The Steatoda spider was given anesthesia and painted blue and red.

The live grasshoppers that were used in The Mummy were chilled in a refrigerator to make them more sluggish.

All of the clocks in Pulp Fiction are stuck on 4:20.

Jeremy Renner prepared for his role as Hawkeye by training with Olympic archers.

Chris Evans had a beard in the post credits scene of The Avengers - it was covered by a prosthetic and by his hands.

Cost of the Spiderman costume for the 2002 movie? $100,000 each. 4 of them were stolen and never returned.

The main characters initials in The Prestige spell Abra (like abracadabra).

The main characters first initials in Inception spell DREAMS.

Mercedes asked that its logo be removed from Slumdog Millionaire scenes that took place in the slums. They thought it would taint the brand.

T2 Arnold Schwarzeneggers per word pay day? $21,429. He spoke a total of 700 words in the movie.

Can you imagine Richard Gere as John McClane?

Billy Crystal took the part of Mike in Monster's Inc after turning down Toy Story the "worst decision of his career".

Christopher Lee is the only member of the Lord Of The Rings crew to meet Tolkien.

Christopher Lee recorded a metal album at the age of 90.

Beverly Hills Cop made up "satellite tracking systems" for the movie. Today we have GPS.

The S.H.I.E.L.D research facility in the Avenger's is NASA's Plum Brook Station.

What would the Man Of Steel had been like if Ben Affleck Directed it?

Casino Royale was the first Bond film approved by Chinese Sensors.

The Ferrari in Ferris Bueller's Day Off is an MG with a fiberglass Ferrari body.

The longest kiss on film? "You're In The Army Now" made in 1941 it lasted 3 minutes and 4 seconds.

George Clooney played Sparky the gay dog in South Park.

Jack Nicholson hasn't appeared on a talk show since 1971. He hates giving interviews.

Sean Connery wore a toupee in every bond film he starred in.

Meryl Streep holds the record for most Golden Globe wins - 7.

Tom Cruise - Best Picture (Rain Man) and Worst Picture (Cocktail) both in 1988.

Dan Akroyd was inspired to write Ghostbusters because of his family's interest in the paranormal.

Eddie Murphy turned down the role of Winston to star in Beverly Hills Cop.

Ivan Reitman voiced both Slimer and Zuul.

Helena Bonham Carter, Sarah Jessica Parker, Jane Krakowski, Laura Dern, and Marisa Tomei all auditioned for the role of Sarah in Labyrinth.

Labyrinth was the final film Jim Henson directed before his untimely death.

John Hughes was inspired to write Sixteen Candles after he received a headshot of Molly Ringwald.

Viggo Mortensen was almost cast as Jake Ryan.

The cake in the iconic final scene of The Sixteen Candles was made out of cardboard.

The original title for The Breakfast Club was Detention.

John Cusack was almost cast in the role of Bender before it eventually went to Judd Nelson.

The library where the Breakfast Club gang serves detention in the film was actually a converted high school gymnasium.

Over 10,000 books were used to set-dress the library. The books were donated by the Chicago Public Library.

Brad Pitt was intended to play the role of Tommy Williams in The Shawshank Redemption

Anthony Michael Hall's real-life mother and sister play his character Brian's mother and sister in the film.

John Hughes made a cameo at the end of The Breakfast Club; he played Brian's father.

Robert Downey Jr. was considered for the role of Duckie in Pretty in Pink.

Steven Spielberg's original concept for E.T. was the story of a family that is terrorized in their home by five aliens.

Harrison Ford's cameo as Elliott's principal was cut from the film.

Disney rejected the script for Back to the Future because of the incestuous storyline involving Marty McFly's mother falling in love with him.

Eric Stoltz was originally cast as Marty McFly.

Doc Brown was originally supposed to have a pet chimpanzee, not a dog.

The iconic DeLorean time machine was originally envisioned as a time travel chamber that resembled a refrigerator.

Both Mickey Rourke and Sylvester Stallone turned down the role of Axel Foley in Beverly Hills Cop before it eventually went to Eddie Murphy.

Beverly Hills Cop wasn't only the highest grossing film of 1984, it was also the highest-grossing R-rated movie of all time, until The Matrix Reloaded kicked it out of the top spot in 2003.

Burt Reynolds turned down the role of Garrett Breedlove in Terms of Endearment

Before casting Julia Roberts in the role of Shelby in Steel Magnolias, producers considered both Winona Ryder and Meg Ryan.

Pat Morita was originally turned down for the role of Mr. Miyagi in The Karate Kid

Before casting Ralph Macchio as Daniel LaRusso, the role was turned down by Charlie Sheen.

Three Men and a Baby is actually a remake of a 1985 French film, 3 hommes et un couffin (Three Men and a Cradle).

Vans became a national shoe brand after Sean Penn's character in Fast Times at Ridgemont High

Ben Stein's classic economics lecture scene was completely improvised and done in one take.

The Princess Bride's director, Rob Reiner, auditioned over 500 women for the role of Buttercup, including Courtney Cox, Meg Ryan, and Uma Thurman

During the filming of The Goonies, Jeff Cohen (Chunk) came down with a case of the chicken pox

Jeff Cohen was so scared he was going to be replaced that he secretly showed up to work sick, and his chicken pox are visible during the iconic "Truffle Shuffle" scene.

Richard Gere took the role of Julian Kaye in American Gigolo two weeks before production started, after John Travolta (who was originally tied to the role) dropped out.

Jennifer Connelly and Justine Bateman were the original choices to play Veronica in Heathers

In the original script for Gremlins, Gizmo was supposed to be the villain, turning into the gremlin Stripe and becoming the leader of the gremlin pack

Tim Burton almost directed Gremlins, but was eventually passed over because he had never directed a feature length film.

Dick Grayson/Robin was originally supposed to appear in a small scene, played by Kiefer Sutherland, but the scene was cut as the filmmakers felt he was irrelevant to the plot.

The Punisher Short Dirty laundry was the first medium to reveal the new punisher logo designed by Tim Bradstreet.

To enhance the scale of the space jockey alien, Ridley Scott filmed kids in miniature space suits.

Psycho - the first american film to show a toilet being flushed.

Darth Vader has 12 minutes of screen time in A New Hope.

Linda Hamilton's twin sister was in T2 - She played the T1000 at the end of the movie.

In Home Alone, Buzz's girlfriend is actually a boy in a wig.

Michael Caine forgot his lines in The Dark Knight when his character meets the Joker for the first time.

Dan Akroyd was in Indiana Jones and the Temple of Doom - he helped Indy board the doomed plane.

Joe Pesci bit Macauly Culkin when filming Home Alone - Macauly still has the scar.

Sean Connery is only 12 years older than Harrison Ford.

The mask used by Michael Myers in Halloween was a Captain Kirk mask.

The slow motion sound effect that was used in Dredd? - It's a Bieber song slowed down 800 times.

Geoffrey Rush requested to be on the left of every shot in Pirates Of the Caribbean, because we read left to right and it would make him look better compared to his pretty co-stars.

The Police officer from hook? Phil Collins - sussudio!

Michelle Pfeiffer had to be vacuum sealed into her Catwoman costume.

Allen Klein gave his song that is used at the end of The Big Lebowski for free

Allen Klein was watching the movie and got to the "I hate the fuckin Eagles, man" scene and made his decision right then.

Machete Don't Text - actual conversation between Danny Trejo and Robert Rodriguez.

The word Dude is used in the Big Lebowski 161 times,
the word Fuck is used 292 times (or variations of it)
and the word man is used 147 times in the Big Lebowski.

Carrie Fisher didn't wear a bra while playing Princess
leia in A New Hope.

Carrie Fishers breasts were duct taped down so she
wouldn't look so feminine.

Carrie Fisher would let random guys from the crew
remove the duct tape after they were finished filming
for the day.

What was the deal with the worst toilet in Scotland
scene in Trainspotting? The bathroom was coated in
chocolate to make it look like the mess it was supposed
to be. Problem? It was chocolate and "smelled
delicious".

Alec Baldwin's character in GlenGarry Glen Ross was
added to the movie to lengthen it.

In Highlander, to get the swords to spark, wires were
run from car batters down the actors sleeves.

Roy Scheider ad libbed the "you're gonna need a bigger
boat" line.

R2-D2 and C3p0 are in every Indiana Jones movie.

Malcom McDowell is terrified of reptiles. Stanley
Kubrick took advantage of it in A Clockwork Orange.

Christopher Lee was part of the League Of Ungentlemanly
Warfare. Secret agent man.

Wookiee suits are made from human hair. all. of. them.

The original raw footage of Apocalypse Now consisted of
1,250,00 ft. of film - 230 hours worth

George Lucas was a cameraman on Apocalypse Now.

George Lucas was originally going to direct Apocalypse
Now

George Lucas envisioned Apocalypse Now to originally be a comedy. It was retitled American Graffiti.

Walt Disney refused to let Alfred Hitchcock film at Disneyland because of "that disgusting movie Psycho"

Peter Sellers was paid 55% of Dr. Strangelove's film budget or 1 million dollars.

Django Unchained was the first time in 16 years that Leonardo DiCaprio didn't get top billing.

Samuel L. Jackson used the words mother fucker to get over his stammer/stutter.

James Earl Jones also had an incredibly bad stutter.

The director of Cannibal Holocaust had to prove in court that the actors were still alive and weren't killed during the movie.

Cannibal Holocaust actors were in seclusion to give the illusion that the film was "real".

Cannibal holocaust is considered the first "found footage" movie.

Supposedly Lance, the drug dealer in Pulp Fiction was offered to Kurt Cobain - so says Courtney Love.

The carpet in the shining and the carpet in Sids house from Toy Story are very similar...

Ryan Goslin was cast in The Notebook because the director wanted someone that was "not handsome".

Drive director Nicolas Winding Refn failed his driving test eight times.

The voice of Barbie in Toy Story? It's Ariel from The Little Mermaid.

Porn Star Asia Carrera and Tara Reid were in the film within a film "Logjammin" from The Big Lebowski.

Sigourney Weaver actually made the basketball shot in Aliens:Resurrection.

Fox passed on The Watchmen it was 'one of the most unintelligble pieces of shit they had read in years".

Wolf Of Wall St. had over four hours of content that had to be cut even further.

Sam Raimi puts his lucky car in all of his films. Including The Quick and the Dead.

Viggo Mortensen was swayed by his son to do The Lord Of The Rings.

Pierce Brosnan was contractually forbidden from wearing a full tuxedo in any non James Bond movie 1995-2002.

The ornaments that Marv steps on in Home Alone - delicious candy.

Charlie Sheen stayed awake for 48 hours to achieve his "wasted" look in Ferris Buellers Day off... really?

Fantasia was originally a short called The Sorcerer's Apprentice. But Walt over spent and didn't want to waste the money.

Sean Connery turned down roles for The Matrix, Lord Of The Rings, Jurassic Park, Indiana Jones 4 and Blade Runner.

Within 3 days The Hunger Games became the highest grossing film for Lionsgate.

Alternate endings - Alien: Resurrection, Ripley makes it back to Earth.

Disney sent Robin Williams a Pablo Picasso painting as a thank you for his work on Aladdin.

Saw was filmed in 18 days.

James Cameron did all the charcoal drawings in Titanic.

Alan Rickman was the only person to know about Snape and Harry Potter's past. Other than Rowling, of course.

Edward Norton was asked to actually hit Brad Pitt in The Fight Club.

Heath Ledger almost broke Jake Gyllenhaal's nose in Brokeback Mountain when they kissed. Muah.

Pixar's UP was the first animated film and 3D film to open the Cannes Film Festival.

The Return Of The King won all 11 Academy Awards it was nominated for.

The 1927 movie Metropolis was supposedly one of Hitler's favorite films.

Original script names - The Sundance Kid and Butch Cassidy.

William Goldman reversed the names when Paul Newman to the role of Butch.

Peter o'Tool was nominated for an Oscar 8 times. He did not win any of them.

Daniel Day-Lewis had to lifted around the set and spoon fed during the production of My Left Foot.

"Warriors, come out to play" was improvised.

Sharlto Copley had no intention of pursuing acting, until District 9.

Each frame of CGI in Cameron's Avatar took about 47 hours to render.

Spirited Away - The only non-western Animated film to win an Oscar for best animated feature.

Paranormal Activity cost $15,000 to make and has made $210 million so far.

In Raiders of the Lost Ark, when Indy shoots the Arab swordsman, he was originally meant to fight him, but Harrison Ford was too ill to fight 'properly.'

The 'Bong' sound/musical cue in Inception is actually the song Non, Je Ne Regrette Rien by Edith Piaf slowed down.

The Shawshank Redemption, #1 on imdb was the 51st highest grossing film in 94', way behind Street Fighter (1994).

Michael Fassbender is to produce and star in an Assassin's Creed movie.

After a slew of drug related offences, Robert Downey Jr. was a semi-blacklisted celebrity until Kiss Kiss Bang Bang reignited his career

Quentin Tarentino was originally going to use the song Wise Man by Frank Ocean in Django Unchained but chose not to

The childish snickering during The Usual Suspects iconic line-up was genuine, caused by Benicio Del Toro's persistent flatulence.

Hasbro denied Pixar the use of GI Joe in Toy Story when found that the GI Joe doll was going to be blown up by Sid.

C.S. Lewis reviewed The Hobbit in 1937 saying, " The Hobbit may well prove a classic."

The floating pen in Kubricks 2001: A Space Odyssey wasn't done with CGI, but camera trickery using glass and tape.

Bryan Cranston (Breaking Bad) played a minor role in Spielbergs 1998, Saving Private Ryan.

Bender from Futurama was named after John Bender from The Breakfast Club.

Ron Jeremy, the pornstar was an extra in Ghostbusters.

In 2002, Steven Spielberg finally finished college after a 33-year hiatus. He turned in Schindler's List for his student film requirement.

On the set of one of the Pirates of the Carribean films, Johnny Depp spent £40,000 on 500 coats for the cast and crew.

On the set of 1982's The Thing, the whole cast and crew was male.

On the first day of filming the exorcism sequence in The Exorcist , Linda Blair's delivery of her foul-mouthed dialogue so disturbed the gentlemanly Max von Sydow forgot his lines.

Peter Ostrum, Charlie from Willy Wonka and the Chocolate Factory, never acted in another movie after that and is now a veterinarian.

In Saving Private Ryan, all of the main cast were given basic military training except Matt Damon, in the hope that the cast would build a resentment towards him necessary for the role.

The Russians made a movie version of The Hobbit in 1985 and it's available on YouTube.

www.ingramcontent.com/pod-product-compliance
Lightning Source LLC
Chambersburg PA
CBHW051859170526
45168CB00001B/175